△ The Triangle Papers: 30

EAST ASIAN SECURITY
AND THE TRILATERAL COUNTRIES

A Report to
The Trilateral Commission

Author: MASASHI NISHIHARA
Professor of International Relations
National Defense Academy of Japan

Special Advisors: JOHN ROPER
Editor, *International Affairs*
Royal Institute of International
Affairs, London

DONALD ZAGORIA
Professor of Government,
Hunter College and
The Graduate Center of the
City University of New York

Published by
NEW YORK UNIVERSITY PRESS
New York and London
1985

This report was prepared for the Trilateral Commission and is released under its auspices. It was discussed at the Trilateral Commission meeting in Tokyo on April 21-23, 1985. The author, who is an expert from Japan, has been free to present his own views; and the opinions expressed are put forth in a personal capacity and do not purport to represent those of the Commission or of any organization with which the author is associated. The Commission is making this report available for wider distribution as a contribution to informed discussion and handling of the issues treated.

© Copyright, 1985. The Trilateral Commission

Library of Congress Cataloging-in-Publication Data
Nishihara, Masashi
  East Asian security and the trilateral countries.

  (The Triangle papers ; 30)
  1. East Asia—National security. 2. East Asia—Relations—Europe. 3. Europe—Rela-
tions—East Asia. 4. East Asia—Relations—United States. 5. United States—Rela-
tions—East Asia. 6. East Asia—Relations—Japan. 7. Japan—Relations—East Asia.
  I. Trilateral Commission.   II. Title.   III. Series.
DS511.N57 1985   950   85-24503
ISBN 0-8147-5758-8
ISBN 0-8147-5759-6 (pbk.)
  Manufactured in the United States of America

THE TRILATERAL COMMISSION

345 East 46th Street   c/o Japan Center for   35, avenue de Friedland
New York, N.Y. 10017   International Exchange   75008 Paris, France
                              4-9-17 Minami-Azabu
                                  Minato-ku
                                 Tokyo, Japan

The Author

MASASHI NISHIHARA is Professor of International Relations at the National Defense Academy. After graduation from Kyoto University's Department of Law in 1962, he entered the University of Michigan, from which he received M.A. and Ph.D. degrees in Political Science. Professor Nishihara has served for Kyoto University's Center for Southeast Asian Studies in Jakarta; has taught at Kyoto Sangyo University and the University of South Carolina; and was a Visiting Research Fellow at the Rockefeller Foundation from 1981 to 1982. He is the author of many works on Japan's security and international relations, including recent articles: "Promoting Partnership: Japan and Europe" (1982) and "Expanding Japan's Credible Defense Role" (1984).

*   *   *

JOHN ROPER (Special Advisor) is Editor of *International Affairs*, the quarterly journal of the Royal Institute of International Affairs, and Specialist and Advisor to the House of Lords Sub-Committee on the Future Financing of the European Communities and a consultant to the European Media Institute at the University of Manchester. He attended schools in England, completing his education at Oxford University and the University of Chicago. Entering the British Parliament in 1964 (Labour), he held many posts during his political career, including Parliamentary Private Secretary to the Minister of State, Department of Industry (1978) and Opposition Front Bench Spokesman on Defense until 1980. He is a founding member of the Social Democratic Party and was Chief Whip from 1981 to 1983.

DONALD ZAGORIA (Special Advisor) is Professor of Government at Hunter College and the Graduate Center of the City University of New York. He is also a fellow at the Research Institute on International Change and at the Harriman Institute for Advanced Study of the Soviet Union, both at Columbia University. In recent years Professor Zagoria served as a consultant to both the National Security Council and the East Asian Bureau of the U.S. Department of State. He has written two books, *The Sino-Soviet Conflict* and *Vietnam Triangle*, and edited and contributed to a third, *Soviet Policy in East Asia*. His numerous articles include two recent pieces in *Foreign Affairs*— "The Moscow-Beijing Detente" (Spring 1983) and "China's Quiet Revolution" (Spring 1984)— and an essay on "The Soviet Union and Asia" in the January 1985 *Asian Survey*.

The Trilateral Process

The report which follows is the responsibility of its author, Masashi Nishihara. He has been especially helped on the European side by John Roper and on the North American side by Donald Zagoria. Mr. Roper and Professor Zagoria commented on outlines and drafts, provided relevant materials, and helped orchestrate Professor Nishihara's consultations in Western Europe and North America.

Masashi Nishihara's primary consultations in Europe took place in October 1984. He participated in the Europe-Japan "Hakone Meeting" in Italy in mid-October, and also had consultations in Rome, Paris, London, and Bonn. He returned to London briefly in February 1985 for consultations with John Roper and with a group of experts drawn together at Chatham House to discuss his first draft. Professor Nishihara was in the United States for consultative meetings in New York on February 19 and in Washington on February 20, supplemented by a few additional appointments. In Ottawa on February 25, his first draft was discussed with a group of government experts from Canada's Department of External Affairs and Department of National Defence, and also with a more academic group gathered at Carleton University. Within Japan, useful materials and advice were provided by a range of officials and others through numerous informal consultations. Useful ideas from persons from other countries in East Asia came especially in the context of the "Asian Dialogue" conference in Tokyo in July 1984 (organized by the Japan Center for International Exchange) and the conference in Seoul in December 1984 on regional security issues (organized by the International Institute for Strategic Studies). The various persons consulted by the author spoke for themselves as individuals and not as representatives of any institutions with which they are associated.

Brian Bridges, *Royal Institute of International Affairs*

Zbigniew Brzezinski, *Senior Adviser, Georgetown University Center for Strategic and International Affairs*

Peter Dobell, *Director, Parliamentary Centre for Foreign Affairs and Foreign Trade, Ottawa*

Reinhard Drifte, *Deputy Director, International Institute for Strategic Studies*

George S. Franklin, *Former Coordinator, The Trilateral Commission; former Executive Director, Council on Foreign Relations*

Ellen Frost, *Director of Japanese Programs, Westinghouse*

John G: Hadwen, *Director-General, Asia and Pacific Branch, Canadian Department of External Affairs*

Charles B. Heck, *North American Director, The Trilateral Commission*

Roger Hill, *Secretary to the Canadian Group of the Trilateral Commission*

Alan Jones, *Policy Development Bureau, Political and Strategic Analysis Division, Canadian Department of External Affairs*

Michael Leifer, *Lecturer, London School of Economics and Political Science*

Winston Lord, *President, Council on Foreign Relations*

Kishore Mahbubhani, *Singaporean Ambassador to the United Nations*

Hanns Maull, *Assistant Professor of Political Science, University of Munich*

Wolf Mendl, *King's College, University of London*

Charles Morrison, *Scholar in Residence, Japan Center for International Exchange; Senior Fellow, East-West Center, University of Hawaii*

Daniel Newman, *Program Assistant to the North American Director, The Trilateral Commission*

Makito Noda, *Program Officer, Japan Center for International Exchange*

Egidio Ortona, *European Deputy Chairman, The Trilateral Commission; Chairman, Honeywell Information Systems Italia*

Didier Pineau-Valencienne, *Chairman, Groupe Schneider, Paris*

Paul Revay, *European Director, The Trilateral Commission*

Francois de Rose, *Ambassadeur de France*

Shiro Saito, *Royal Institute for International Affairs*

Yukio Sato, *Former Japanese Consul-General, London*

Lord Shackleton, *Rio-Tinto Zinc Corporation; former British Cabinet Minister*

Masahide Shibusawa, *Director, East West Seminar*

Cornelius Sommer, *Policy Planning Staff, German Ministry of Foreign Affairs*

Tadashi Yamamoto, *Japanese Director, The Trilateral Commission*

Michael M. Yoshitsu, *North American Deputy Director, The Trilateral Commission*

Other persons consulted by the author, special advisors and regional directors include the following:

Jonathan Alford, *Deputy Director, International Institute for Strategic Studies*

William Barnds, *President, Japan Economic Institute*

A. Doak Barnett, *Professor, The Johns Hopkins School of Advanced International Studies (SAIS)*

R.E. Bedeski, *Professor of Political Science, Carleton University*

Richard Betts, *Senior Fellow, The Brookings Institution*
William Bauer, *Former Canadian Ambassador to the Republic of Korea*
Thomas Bernstein, *Professor of Political Science, Columbia University*
John Bresnan, *Director, The Williamsburg Project, The Asia Society*
Giovanni Bressi, *University of Turin*
Perronne Capano, *Former Italian Ambassador to Japan*
Herve de Carmoy, *Chief Executive, International Midland Bank*
Maurizio Cremasco, *Istituto Affari Internazionali, Rome*
Evelyn Colbert, *Professorial Lecturer, The Johns Hopkins School of Advanced International Studies*
Richard Combs, *Director of Eastern Europe and Yugoslavia Affairs, U.S. Department of State*
Alain Cotta, *Professor of Economics and Management, University of Paris*
Gerald L. Curtis, *Professor of Political Science, Columbia University*
Jean Deflassieux, *Chairman, Credit Lyonnais*
Dick Douglas, *Member of British Parliament*
Mark Elliot, *Head of the Far Eastern Department, Foreign and Commonwealth Office*
H.E. English, *Department of Economics, Carleton University*
Banning Garret, *Co-Director, Strategic Policy Analysis, Palomar Corporation*
Michel Gaudet, *International Chamber of Commerce*
Bonnie Glaser, *Co-Director, Strategic Policy Analysis, Palomar Corporation*
Michio Hamano, *Embassy of Japan to Canada*
Han Sung-Joo, *Director, Asiatic Research Center, Korea University*
Erland Heginbotham, *Staff Member, Senate Committee on Foreign Relations*
Stephane Hessel, *Ambassadeur de France*
Terence Higgins, *Member of British Parliament*
Karl Kaiser, *Director of the Research Institute of the German Society for Foreign Affairs*
Paul Kreisberg, *Director of Studies, Council on Foreign Relations*
Robert Legvold, *Associate Director, W. Averell Harriman Institute for Advanced Study of the Soviet Union, Columbia University*
John Malott, *Acting Director for Japanese Affairs, U.S. Department of State*
Rod McDougall, *U.S. Programs Division, Canadian Department of External Affairs*
Ogay Mehmet, *Professor of Administration, Ottawa University*
Cesare Merlini, *Chairman, Istituto Affari Internazionali, Rome*

Mike Mochizuki, *Assistant Professor of Political Science, Yale University*

Thierry de Montbrial, *Director, French Institute for International Affairs*

Larry A. Niksch, *Congressional Research Service*

Sadako Ogata, *Professor of International Relations, Sophia University*

Robert O'Neill, *Director, International Institute for Strategic Studies*

Hugh Patrick, *Robert D. Calkins Professor, Columbia University School of Business*

Gunter Poser, *Retired Rear Admiral, German Navy*

Robert Pranger, *Director of International Programs, American Enterprise Institute*

Sean Randolph, *Deputy to Ambassador Richard Fairbanks, U.S. Department of State*

Sir Julian Ridsdale, *Member of British Parliament*

Martin Rudner, *Associate Professor of Development Studies, Carleton University*

A. William Scully, *Legislative Assistant, Office of Senator William Roth*

Paul Shaw, *Professor, The Norman Paterson School of International Affairs, Carleton University*

Gaston Sigur, *Director of Asian Affairs, U.S. National Security Council*

Stefano Silvestri, *Deputy Chairman, Istituto Affari Internazionali, Rome*

A.S. Simard, *Director, Pacific Relations Division, Canadian Department of External Affairs*

Richard Sneider, *Former U.S. Ambassador to the Republic of Korea*

Cornelius Sommer, *Policy Planning Staff, German Ministry of Foreign Affairs*

John Stremlau, *Acting Director, International Relations, The Rockefeller Foundation*

Elliot Tepper, *Professor of Political Science, Carleton University*

Vincenzo Tornetta, *Former Italian Ambassador to Vietnam, Japan, and NATO*

Paolo Battino Vittorelli, *Chairman, ISTRID, Rome*

Angelika Volle, *Research Institute of the German Society for Foreign Affairs*

Somsakdi Xuto, *Professor, National Institute of Development Administration, Bangkok*

The author wishes to thank in particular Makito Noda, Program Officer of the Japan Center for International Exchange, who helped the author prepare various tables in the text as well as in the appendix and contributed actively to task force deliberations.

Table of Contents

* * *

Tables

Introduction

Today, for the trilateral countries of North America, Western Europe, and Japan, the security of the East Asian region, including both Northeast and Southeast Asia, is increasingly important, both in its own right and for its connection with global security. The growing Soviet military deployments in the East Asian and Pacific region threaten the security positions of the United States and Japan, with which the countries of Western Europe have crucial ties. China, the most populated developing nation with nuclear capabilities, and Japan, a non-nuclear nation with great economic and technological capabilities, play more important roles in shaping the regional and global order than ever before.

The nations of Northeast and Southeast Asia[1] have a combined population of about 1,500 million, nearly one-third of the world's total, and are also economically dynamic. South Korea, Taiwan, Hong Kong, and Singapore have the world's highest rate of economic growth and frequently are referred to as NICs, newly industrialized countries. Other members of the Association of Southeast Asian Nations (ASEAN) follow closely. The economic dynamism of Northeast and Southeast Asia has enhanced political stability and offered attractive economic opportunities for the trilateral countries. But at the same time, countries in the region are competing with the trilateral nations in certain important industrial sectors such as textiles, television sets, shipbuilding, and microcomputers. They threaten the equivalent sectors of the North American, European, and Japanese economies. A shift to protectionism in the trilateral countries could bring to a halt the economic growth of the region and its political benefits. The economic success of East Asia has popularized the concept of "the Pacific Basin Community," raising "the Atlantic versus Pacific" debate. There are fears in some segments of Western Europe that U.S. attention may be diverted from Europe to Asia, thus weakening the trans-Atlantic relationship and affecting trilateral security.

Because most East Asian nations have only limited experience in managing modern governments, they still lack mature political institutions, a situation which is reflected in personalized authoritarian lead-

---

[1]Covered in this report are China, Japan, Hong Kong, North and South Korea, and Taiwan for Northeast Asia; Burma, Kampuchea, Laos, Vietnam, and the six ASEAN nations (Brunei, Indonesia, Malaysia, the Philippines, Singapore, and Thailand) for Southeast Asia. The Soviet Far East is also treated as part of Northeast Asia.

ership, coups d'etat, and political suppression. The rules of political succession have still to be established or confirmed through practice in most countries in the region. Furthermore, the multi-ethnic character of most societies in Southeast Asia carries the potential for inter-communal tensions, while their cultural heterogeneity generates social divisions such as those between Western-educated secular pragmatists and indigenous religious fundamentalists. These elements of political tension tend to undermine the political stability of the developing countries of East Asia, making them a potentially attractive target for interference by external powers. Political turmoil in the non-Communist parts of the region (as in the Philippines) may weaken the strategic interests of the United States in the region and may affect the political and economic positions of the other trilateral governments. Should such internal political troubles spill over into international regional and global relationships, they could become a focal point of East-West tensions and affect the security of all the trilateral countries.

The growing significance of the East Asian region requires a fresh examination of the questions that the Trilateral Commission countries face today: How does the security of East Asia affect trilateral interests, individually and collectively, and how should the trilateral countries respond to such threats, individually and collectively? What factors are promoting or damaging trilateral security interests? What differences among trilateral policies toward the region are adversely affecting their interests and thus need to be resolved through closer consultation and coordination? There exists a large literature on the interests and roles of the United States and Japan in East Asia, but there are few references to Canadian and Western European interests and involvements, and even fewer discussions of the link between East Asia's security and the *common* interests of the trilateral countries. Hence this report.

After presenting an overall picture of the security environment of East Asia in Chapter I, the report reviews the postwar transformation of trilateral interests and involvements in the region in Chapter II. Chapter III discusses the current interests of the trilateral nations in East Asia and their perceptions of strategic factors in the region. Next follow three chapters analyzing the new strategic situation in East Asia, elements of regional instability, and the prospects for arms control in the region. The final chapter discusses certain implications of these security issues for security in the trilateral countries and makes recommendations for the trilateral nations concerning their policies toward East Asia.

I. THE SECURITY ENVIRONMENT OF EAST ASIA: AN OVERALL PICTURE

A. BALANCE OF POWER THAT FAVORS THE NON-COMMUNIST SIDE

The balance of power in East Asia, both strategic and regional, on the whole favors the non-Communists. In the postwar years international relations in East Asia have been bipolarized to varying degrees. The current phase of bipolarization emerged after the fall of Saigon in 1975 and especially when the United States, Japan, China, South Korea, the ASEAN nations, Australia, and New Zealand formed a loose coalition in response to the November 1978 Moscow-Hanoi Treaty of Friendship and Cooperation and the subsequent Vietnamese invasion of Kampuchea. Practically all the nations in East Asia took sides on this question by the early 1980s. Then, from late 1982, a crack in the wall of bipolarization appeared in Northeast Asia as China began to emphasize an "independent" foreign policy and to normalize relations with the Soviet Union while North Korea began to tilt more clearly toward Beijing.

Despite its new posture, China wants to be regarded as a power friendly to the non-Communist countries of the Pacific rim. China and the United States conduct strategic consultations on Soviet power. They cooperate in security matters through arms sales, the exchange of visits by high-ranking military officers, and it is widely reported that there are U.S. posts in China monitoring Soviet military activity. Because of China's position involving closer relations with the United States than the Soviet Union, the U.S. position in the East Asian balance is better than the Soviet one.

The non-Communist side also maintains an edge in the regional balance. The United States at present maintains bilateral security treaties with Japan, South Korea, and the Philippines. It abrogated its security treaty with the Republic of China at the end of 1979, but domestic legislation (the Taiwan Relations Act of January 1979) obliges it to supply "defensive" arms to Taiwan. The Southeast Asia Treaty Organization (SEATO) was dissolved in 1977, but the Manila Treaty of 1954, to which the United States and Britain are parties, is still valid. This treaty is the legal basis for the U.S. defense commitment to Thailand. The U.S. is also widening security contacts with the ASEAN nations through arrangements short of treaties such as arms sales, officer training, joint maneuvers, and the like. It has an indirect security relationship with Singapore and Malaysia, because the latter two Southeast Asian nations are parties to the Five-Power Defense Arrangement (FPDA) of 1971, together with Britain, Australia, and New Zealand, with which the United States maintains security treaties through NATO and ANZUS. The current strain between Washington and Wellington over the latter's refusal to permit U.S. nuclear-armed and nuclear-powered warships to make port visits will probably not weaken ANZUS seriously. Thus, the Soviet military presence in Vietnam notwithstanding, both the strategic and regional balance of power in East Asia still favors the non-Communist side.

How long is this relatively favorable security environment likely to last, and what are the major factors which might change it? Three essential elements need to be borne in mind in discussing the regional security environment: (1) East Asia has become more and more important geostrategically for the two superpowers; (2) East Asia has been and continues to be a region where internal conflicts could affect global security; and (3) the continued economic growth of East Asia could have negative as well as positive consequences for regional security.

B. GEOSTRATEGIC IMPORTANCE FOR THE SUPERPOWERS

East Asia, coupled with the Western Pacific, is one area where the Soviet Union is actively challenging the U.S. global and regional military position. The Soviet Union claims to be an Asia-Pacific power, as does the United States. This kind of contest for hegemony is not unusual in East Asia, considering its geostrategic importance. Historically, all major world powers have aspired to attain spheres of influence there. Before the Asian colonial power, Japan, came to dominate the region briefly during World War II, European colonial powers had come to the region in succession: the Spanish in the Philippines; the Dutch in Indonesia (Netherlands East Indies); the British in Burma, Malaysia, Singapore, and Hong Kong; and the French in Indochina. The Americans were latecomers as a colonial power, but succeeded in driving out Spanish rule from Manila at the beginning of the present century and in entering China to compete with British, French, German, and Japanese bids for colonial expansion in that country. The Germans also took over the Central Pacific islands.

This is not the place to review the post-World War II history of international relations in East Asia; however, the past struggles among the major powers to dominate the region confirm the geostrategic as well as the economic challenge of East Asia. For the United States as a global seapower, the security of the sea lanes of communications (SLOC) linking the Pacific and the Indian Oceans has been of strategic importance. To ensure the security of the sea lanes, the United States has sought to gain friendly ports in Northeast and Southeast Asia and to neutralize any potential hostile forces that may threaten the use of those ports and the Pacific-Indian Ocean SLOC.

Today, the geostrategic importance of East Asia for the United States is greater than ever before. The reason is simply that the Soviet Union considers the East Asia-Pacific region to be more important geostrategically than ever before. The Soviet Union now deploys one-quarter to one-third of its entire forces and arms in its Far East region and the Western Pacific Ocean. Its strategic nuclear forces operating from Petropavlovsk, Kamchatka, and underwater in the Sea of Okhotsk can now directly strike the American continent. Also, the development of Siberia, which has been given greater priority in recent years, requires that the Soviet Far East be secure.

The region's security is particularly important to the Soviet Union, given the fact that the sparsely populated Far East region shares long borders with the heavily populated Northeast region (formerly Manchuria) of potentially hostile China and that serious armed clashes did occur in that very area in 1969. The increasing contacts between the United States and China and between Japan and China in recent years, particularly in 1983 and 1984, worry Moscow greatly. For some time Moscow has sought to encircle China. In 1969, in an effort to do so, General Secretary Brezhnev proposed an "Asian collective security system" for Asian nations. Though he succeeded in setting up security arrangements only with India (in 1971), Vietnam (in 1978) and Afghanistan (in 1979), the Soviet use of military facilities in Danang and Cam Rahn Bay that began after 1978 has strengthened Moscow's political as well as strategic position vis-a-vis Washington and Beijing. The Soviet-Vietnamese alliance has added another important element to Moscow's global strategy and enables it to project its power into the Indian Ocean. This threatens the U.S. strategic interest in maintaining the security of SLOC between the Pacific and Indian Oceans.

C. A REGION OF POTENTIAL GLOBAL CONFLICTS

Unlike the situation in Europe, the dividing line between a Soviet sphere and a Western sphere was never sharply defined in East Asia. The presence of nonaligned countries and weak governments made parts of East Asia focal points of intense East-West competition. This was especially true of divided nations, of which there were three in East Asia. In China, the 1945-49 civil war resulted in a Communist victory without major external intervention. However, in Korea (1950-53) and Vietnam (1945-54 and 1961-73), efforts to unify these countries resulted in outside intervention, the intensification of warfare, and the potential for further escalation. In point of fact, in both cases, the superpowers were careful to limit the warfare, both to conventional weapons and to the countries involved. There were no direct confrontations of the military forces of the two superpowers.

That future conflicts in Asia would necessarily follow the same pattern should not be taken for granted. Fragile governments, divided nations, and the potential for serious communal or ethnic conflicts carry with them the seeds of domestic struggle and the possibility of outside intervention. As economic growth has increased the stakes in Asia and as the military capabilities of the superpowers have become more equal, there is a possibility that domestic conflicts in the region could ignite a broader war.

Compared with postwar Europe, power realignments seem to be the norm rather than the exception in East Asia. At least four major realignments have occurred in the region in the postwar period. First, the staunch wartime enemy of the United States, Japan, has become its ally and its wartime friend, the Soviet Union, has become its adversary. Second, Indonesia, the largest and most populous nation in Southeast Asia, was "an axis" with China from 1963 to 1965 when it abruptly cut off relations because of the alleged complicity of Beijing's Communist Party in the ill-fated Communist coup. Indonesia then sought close ties with the industrialized democracies. Third, China broke away during the 1960s from its one-time ally, the Soviet Union, and has sought a cooperative relationship with the United States since the 1970s. Fourth, China and Vietnam, long-time allies in the war against U.S. imperialism, ruptured their relations in 1978 and even fought a war in the following year. East Asia has thus drastically redrawn its political map several times during the past four decades.

By no means can it be said that revisions of the region's political map have ended. The current war in Kampuchea between anti-Vietnamese forces supported by China and the ASEAN nations on one hand and Vietnamese and Hanoi-backed Kampuchean forces on the other may produce a new political map. Soviet-Vietnamese relations show some signs of strain which may increase in the future. International power relations over the Korean question are also potentially fluid, as both North and South Korea are seeking contacts with their respective adversaries. The political instability of the Marcos government in Manila could bring to power anti-Washington political forces, creating tense relations with the United States. Other possible shifts could be precipitated by the Taiwan question or territorial disputes in the South China Sea. These points will be discussed later at greater length.

Power realignments occur not just by the force of international power relations. They are often engendered as the consequence of internal factors such as Communist subversives, inter-ethnic conflicts, religious tensions, economic disparities, leadership succession, and technological changes. East Asia appears to have an environment susceptible to armed conflicts. Most regional and local conflicts may be contained as they have been in the past. But two possible conflicts which could have immediate global security dimensions are a second Korean War or a significant Sino-Soviet border clash. In addition, in 1982 Japan depended upon imports of energy for 83 percent of its energy requirements and upon the Persian Gulf area for 71 percent of its crude oil imports. Conflicts involving the Soviet Union, the United States, and Japan would be likely to be an immediate consequence if there were a general war in Europe or in the Gulf. In this sense, East Asia is a region of potential global conflict.

D. A REGION OF SUSTAINED ECONOMIC GROWTH

Another important factor to be kept in mind in discussing the security environment of East Asia is the relatively high economic growth which the region's non-Communist nations enjoy and the importance of this phenomenon for political stability. Between 1978 and 1982 the nine non-Communist countries of East Asia maintained an average annual GNP growth rate of 7.0 percent whereas the annual growth rates of countries in the European Community (EC) and North America were 1.5 percent and 1.6 percent respectively. In the ten years since 1973, per capita GNP for the East Asian non-Communist countries increased from $1,210 to $3,038 in nominal terms (see Table 1). In particular, Japan and the NICs maintained average growth rates of 10.4 percent and 13.6 percent respectively. Japan's per capita GNP grew from $3,807 to $9,696, and that of the NICs from $632 to $2,552 in the last ten years (see Table 2).

Sustained economic growth is not a sufficient condition for political stability, but certainly a necessary condition for it. Not all East Asian countries can claim that they have retained political stability. Most of the economically successful governments of the region have been run by strong leaders who have stayed in power for so long that they have often faced the problem of political legitimacy. One example is Presi-

East Asian Security

TABLE 1

**Growth of Nominal Per Capita GNP in Non-Communist
East Asian Countries, 1973-83**
(in current U.S. dollars)

	1973	1978	1983	% GROWTH BETWEEN 1973 AND 1983
Burma*	103.7	143.7	170.1	64.0%
Hong Kong*	1,802.3	3,764.6	5,316.1	195.0%
Indonesia	124.3	347.7	474.3	281.6%
Japan	3,806.8	8,383.4	9,696.2	154.7%
ROK	386.6	1,281.0	1,885.9	387.8%
Malaysia	654.5	1,154.7	1,849.6	182.6%
Philippines	264.8	527.7	658.2	148.6%
Singapore	1,865.2	3,314.5	6,440.7	245.3%
Taiwan	679.6	1,538.5	2,668.3	292.6%
Thailand	266.2	513.7	793.3	198.0%
Weighted Average	1,209.8	2,621.8	3,037.8	151.1%

*per capita GDP
Source: Produced on the basis of the International Monetary Fund's *International Financial
Statistics,* and the Asian Development Bank's *Key Indicators of Developing Member
Countries of ADB.*

TABLE 2

**Growth of Nominal Per Capita GNP in Non-Communist
East Asian Region, 1973-83**
(in current U.S. dollars)

	(a)1973	1978	(b)1983	$\dfrac{(b)-(a)}{(a)}$%
East Asia[1]	1,209.8	2,621.8	3,037.8	151.1%
ANICs[2]	632.2	1,618.7	2,551.8	303.6%
ASEAN[3]	155.9	481.8	692.9	344.5%
Japan	3,806.8	8,383.4	9,696.2	154.7%

[1] Weighted average of Burma, Hong Kong, Indonesia, Japan, ROK, Malaysia, Philippines, Singapore, Taiwan and Thailand.
[2] Weighted average of Hong Kong, ROK, Singapore and Taiwan.
[3] Weighted average of Indonesia, Malaysia, Philippines, Singapore and Thailand.

Source: Produced on the basis of the International Monetary Fund's *International Financial
Statistics* and the Asian Development Bank's *Key Indicators of Developing Member
Countries of ADB.*

TABLE 3

Trade Balances of Japan and Asian NICs vis-a-vis Trilateral Countries

(in million U.S. dollars)

	JAPAN				U.S.				CANADA				WESTERN EUROPE			
	1980	1981	1982	1983	1980	1981	1982	1983	1980	1981	1982	1983	1980	1981	1982	1983
Hong Kong	−4,233	−4,734	−4,235	−4,550	2,504	3,467	3,502	4,432	237	309	307	435	1,882	1,298	996	851
ROK	−2,819	−2,871	−1,900	−2,963	−266	−362	329	1,806	−34	−47	−40	187	1,230	946	1,522	1,042
Singapore	−2,751	−3,064	−2,782	−3,067	−964	−713	−1,020	−307	4	52	31	59	−481	−713	−1,294	−1,092
Taiwan	−3,180	−3,450	−2,402	−3,107	2,087	3,397	4,196	6,687	211	300	184	367	2,110	1,926	−800	491
Total	−12,983	−14,119	−11,319	−13,687	3,361	5,789	7,007	12,618	418	614	482	1,048	4,741	3,457	424	1,292
Japan					6,959	13,312	12,151	18,182	−2,287	−1,065	−1,580	−805	11,045	12,122	11,464	12,048

Source: Produced on the basis of figures presented in the Asian Development Bank's *Key Indicators of Developing Member Countries of ADB* (April 1984 and October 1984).

dent Park Chung Hee of South Korea who was challenged by Kim Dae Jun in 1971 and finally assassinated by the KCIA director in 1979. To a lesser degree, President Suharto of Indonesia and President Ferdinand Marcos of the Philippines suffer from the legitimacy issue or what is sometimes called "regime fatigue." In East Asia, economic growth, a source of political stability today, could be a source of political instability tomorrow, if those in power were considered to promote economic growth for their own benefit rather than to try to close the widening gap between rich and poor.

Competitive goods produced by the high-growth economies of East Asia also have created trade friction with North American and European countries. In 1983, Japan and the four NICs had trade surpluses of $30.8 billion with the United States, $0.2 billion with Canada, and $13.3 billion with the EC, or a total surplus of $44.3 billion with these three regions (see Table 3). In particular, Japan's trade surplus amounted to $18.2 billion with the United States and $12.0 billion with the EC. The trade imbalance between Japan and the United States, which amounted to nearly $37 billion in 1984, is one reason for Washington's increased criticism of Japan's trade and non-tariff barriers and for heightened political tensions that may encourage trade protectionism in the United States.

Japan's trade surplus has also caused conflicts with the developing countries of East Asia, which urge Japan to buy more of their products. This also can become a domestic political issue, with those in power being criticized for their inability to settle the trade issue with Tokyo.

II. PAST TRILATERAL INVOLVEMENTS IN REVIEW

Today, North America, Western Europe, and Japan share a great interest in retaining and strengthening the security positions of the non-Communist countries in East Asia, but this situation is rather new. Because of their differing strategic interests, national strengths, and historical relationships with the region, the trilateral nations have had varying degrees of involvement in East Asian regional affairs in the four postwar decades.

The past four decades can be divided into two periods in terms of the level of convergence of trilateral interests with the dividing point in the mid-1970s. The trend toward a higher level of convergence began after the Vietnam War, and it became clearer by 1978. The Soviet-Vietnamese Treaty of Friendship and Cooperation signed that year crystallized bipolarization in the region, and the trilateral countries were united in support of those countries critical of Vietnam's subsequent aggressive behavior backed by the treaty. During the first period, however, more events occurred over which the trilateral countries took dissonant stands than in the second period when more consonant cases were seen. Also important to note is the fact that during the second period Japan and other non-Communist countries in East Asia began to share more of a strategic consensus with the United States and Western Europe than before.

A. THE PERIOD OF MORE DISSONANT TRILATERAL INVOLVEMENTS: 1945 THROUGH MID-1970S

The period from 1945 through the mid-1970s roughly corresponds to the Cold War and detente years in global East-West relations. Unlike the situation in Europe, the postwar years in East Asia began with a distinctive dissonance in trilateral interests. The United States emerged as the dominant Asia-Pacific power and filled the power vacuum created by the defeat of Imperial Japan. Aware of its global mission, the United States chose to assume primary responsibility for shaping the course of major events in the region, as it did elsewhere. It had its own resources—military, political, and economic—to pursue such perceived responsibilities. Besides, it had the advantage of not having been a colonial power in the region except in the Philippines, whose eventual independence it encouraged rather than resisted. Because of these facts, the United States and its present trilateral partners had divergent interests in the immediate postwar years.

The United States, for instance, almost single-handedly occupied Japan in order to ensure that Japan would never again become "a menace to the United States or to the peace and security of the world," as Washington's initial occupation policy stated. The Japanese were preoccupied with their own political reorientation and economic reconstruction. In 1945 and 1946 some six million Japanese were demobilized and returned home from practically all corners of East Asia as well as the South Pacific. Japan began postwar diplomacy with a guilt complex toward other peoples in the Asia-Pacific region for having forced them to build Japan's sphere of influence called the Greater East Asia Coprosperity Sphere. The United States, Britain, France, Canada, and the Netherlands were on the Far Eastern Commission, created in late 1945, to supervise the Allied Occupation of Japan. In no way were they Japan's partners.

The Americans were uneasy about the French coming back to postwar Indochina to restore their colonial empire. From 1943 until early 1945, President Roosevelt had seriously considered the idea of placing Indochina under an international trusteeship partly to prevent France's return after the war. Initially the United States was on good terms with the Vietnamese Communists led by Ho Chi Minh. Only after the Korean War broke out did the United States begin to provide significant military supplies to France. Yet U.S. sympathy with the anti-French nationalist cause during the early postwar years continued to be a source of tension between the two powers throughout the Vietnam War. Like the French, the Dutch attempted to restore their colonial rule in Indonesia and were challenged by nationalists. Here again it was the United States that intervened and successfully persuaded the Netherlands in 1949 to leave Indonesia. In contrast, there were few disagreements between the United States and Britain on the latter's policy toward its former colonies, as it prepared for a smooth transition of power—in Burma in 1947 and in Malaya in 1957.

The trilateral countries also had differences of approach toward China after Mao Zedong took power in 1949. While the United States decided to continue to support the Republic of China in Taipei and not to recognize the new People's Republic of China (PRC), Britain and small European powers such as Sweden, Denmark, Switzerland, and Finland recognized the PRC as early as 1950, and they were followed in 1954 by Norway and the Netherlands. France recognized the PRC in 1964, just as the Vietnam War began to intensify (see Table 4). These

TABLE 4

Years of Normalization of Diplomatic Relations with China
(Trilateral Countries and East Asia)

	NORTH AMERICA	WEST EUROPE	EAST ASIA AND PACIFIC
1949*			Korea, DPR Mongolia
1950		Sweden Denmark Switzerland Finland UK	Vietnam Burma Indonesia
1954		Norway Netherlands	
1958			Cambodia
1961			Laos
1964		France	
1970	Canada	Italy	
1971		San Marino Austria Belgium Iceland	
1972		Malta Greece Germany, Fed. Rep. Luxembourg	Australia Japan New Zealand
1974			Malaysia
1975			Fiji Philippines Thailand Western Samoa
1976			Papua New Guinea
1979	USA	Ireland Portugal	

*USSR

differences in approach among the trilateral countries remained an issue until the United States made a dramatic move to normalize relations with the PRC. Japan followed the U.S. lead regarding recognition until 1972, but experienced friction with the United States because it conducted trade and exchanged visitors with the PRC.

The Korean War was considered by a majority (53 nations) of United Nations members in 1950 to have started as an act of clear aggression from north of the 38th parallel, and it was relatively easy for the United States, as leader of the free world, to mobilize the support of the other trilateral governments. Fifteen other countries sent combat forces including Belgium, Britain, Canada, France, Greece, Luxembourg, and the Netherlands. These nations lost nearly 1,700 soldiers in combat, while over 54,000 American soldiers lost their lives. Japan also played an important role by giving logistical support to the U.N. forces.

Unlike Korea, both the First and Second Indochina Wars failed to produce a convergence of trilateral interests. In the first war, the United States and Britain disagreed on how the war should be settled. Prior to the fall of Dien Bien Phu in 1954, the former considered for a while a bold plan for allied air strikes against the Viet Minh, but Britain refused to cooperate. Instead the British proposed a negotiated settlement based on partition, a position the French accepted after the Dien Bien Phu defeat. With the Soviet Union, Britain co-chaired the Geneva Conference, to help reduce international tension and to retain its international prestige. But the Americans, interested in containing Communist expansion, were eager to discredit the Geneva cease-fire agreements and refused to sign them. Even before the truce was reached, the United States had prepared to prop up the South Vietnam regime and form the Southeast Asia Treaty Organization (SEATO), in order to deter "the domino effect" of Communist influence. Britain and France became European members of SEATO, but France no longer had an interest in sending troops to the region, while Britain saw that it could benefit primarily because it was fighting Communist subversives in Malay jungles, and because SEATO protection of Thailand, Malaya's northern neighbor, was important. During these years Japan followed the United States lead. But it chose not to get militarily or politically involved, assisting South Vietnam by economic means only.

The Second Indochinese War was heavily Americanized. Major West European countries and Japan supported the American security commitment to South Vietnam in principle, but with many reservations. Political leaders frequently sought to distance themselves from escalation of the U.S. war effort. Britain supported that effort, partly because it needed U.S. support for Malaysia, which Sukarno of Indonesia had declared "a British neocolonialist scheme." When President De Gaulle in 1964 proposed the neutralization of Southeast Asia, especially Indochina, he probably hoped to restore a degree of French political influence to the region. Later, some Nordic countries were havens for U.S. "draft dodgers." All of these actions certainly annoyed the United States.

The 1969 Guam Doctrine, in which the United States declared that the main burden of self-defense should be borne by its allies, provided the basis for the deescalation of U.S. war efforts. This important departure from the earlier U.S. policy of active engagement in Asia led not only to the cease-fire of 1973 and the fall of Saigon in April 1975 but also to the closing of U.S. bases in Thailand the following year. There was little disagreement among the trilateral countries on the application of the Guam Doctrine to Vietnam. The process of the deescalation of the Vietnam War was in fact welcomed in Japan, partly because it facilitated the process for returning Okinawa to Japanese sovereignty, another thorny issue between Tokyo and Washington. However, when President Carter proposed the withdrawal of U.S. ground forces in Korea, both the Japanese and many Southeast Asian governments expressed concern. The tension between Japan and the United States was relieved only when Carter announced in February 1979 that he was freezing his withdrawal plan.

B. THE PERIOD OF MORE CONSONANT TRILATERAL
INVOLVEMENTS:
AFTER THE MID-1970S

In the period after the mid-1970s, the trilateral nations found that they had increasing common interests on certain issues of international significance. The Islamic Revolution in Iran and the Soviet invasion of Afghanistan were certainly among such issues. Where East Asia was concerned, these issues related to China, Indochinese refugees, the ASEAN-Vietnam conflict, and the Soviet military buildup in East Asia. A principal factor behind each was Vietnam's anti-Chinese policy and the resultant Soviet-Vietnamese alliance, which was formalized in November 1978. That year Japan also signed the treaty of peace and friendship with China, while the United States announced it would normalize relations with the PRC after January 1979. The trilateral nations adopted mutually similar postures toward China; there were minor differences in nuance and degree but not in kind. All of the trilateral nations considered China's anti-Soviet policy to be strategically beneficial in maintaining the East-West balance in the latter's favor. They also wanted to encourage China's economic policy shift and to improve their own economic relations with China.

The outflow of Indochinese refugees, which began in 1975 and increased dramatically in 1978, became not only a humanitarian issue but also a grave source of regional insecurity. Neighboring nations— Thailand, Malaysia, Singapore, and Indonesia—struggled to meet the needs of the "boat people" and the "land people" who escaped from Hanoi's socialist transformation programs and compulsory military service and from the Pol Pot regime's holocaust. After early 1979 several international conferences took place in East Asia and Geneva in an effort to find practical solutions to the basic needs of over half a million refugees. Such conferences were attended without exception by the trilateral nations, the ASEAN nations, and Australia. The Tokyo Summit of June 1979 also issued a joint statement with rare Japanese initiatives calling for an early solution of the refugee problem. The Soviet Union and other Communist countries, except China, expressed no interest in extending help. The trilateral countries not only made financial contributions but also accepted the refugees into their own countries for resettlement. Japan was criticized for accepting only a handful of refugees, but its financial contributions were substantial, ultimately defusing this criticism. The trilateral countries also took the dramatic step of either freezing aid to Hanoi or cancelling it entirely in protest of Hanoi's aggression in Kampuchea and the inhumanitarian conditions that gave rise to the refugee outflow.

Tension between the then five ASEAN nations and Vietnam, which was further inflamed after the latter's invasion of Kampuchea in late 1978, not only helped consolidate the ASEAN members but also helped them gain sympathy from the trilateral nations. In his 1977 visit to Southeast Asia, Prime Minister Fukuda had announced that Japan would continue friendly relations with both Indochina and the ASEAN nations. When the conflict over Kampuchea arose, Japan, under ASEAN pressure, revised this so-called Fukuda Doctrine and decided to give political and economic support to the ASEAN side and to be cool to Hanoi. Following the ASEAN-Japan foreign ministers meeting in 1978, the ASEAN foreign ministers conference held in June 1979 concluded joint sessions with counterparts from the United States, Japan, Australia, and New Zealand plus the President of the EC Council of Ministers. Canada also became a regular participant after the 1980 meeting. Meeting with these outside powers has since become a practice at the annual ASEAN foreign ministers conference. The annual enlarged sessions have issued statements strongly condemning Vietnam's military occupation of Kampuchea.

The trilateral nations also cooperated in different international forums with ASEAN efforts to effectuate the withdrawal of Vietnamese forces. At the United Nations the trilateral nations either endorsed or co-sponsored ASEAN-initiated resolutions that backed the continued U.N. membership of the Democratic Kampuchean coalition government formed by the Sihanouk, Sonn San, and Khieu Samphan groups in 1982, and that supported the idea of a demilitarized zone along the Thai-Kampuchean borders and U.N.-administered free elections to bring about a Vietnamese withdrawal and a neutral Kampuchea.

There are two issues concerning Indochina on which the trilateral countries do not agree: whether Democratic Kampuchea should remain recognized and whether Hanoi should be recognized. On the first issue, the United States, West Germany, and France have never recognized Democratic Kampuchea, whereas Japan and most other West European nations have done so. Britain and Australia, however, withdrew recognition in December 1979 and February 1981, respectively, but neither recognized the Vietnamese-backed Heng Samrin government. On the second issue, most of the trilateral countries have had official relations with Hanoi. The United States is a notable exception, although in negotiating the return of American soldiers missing in action, it probably has had the closest, albeit most frustrating, contacts with the Hanoi government. The potential problem arising from these differences among the trilateral countries will be discussed further in subsequent sections.

Finally, the increased Soviet military presence in East Asia solidified the trilateral position on U.S.-Soviet relations. The perceived Soviet threat, especially after the Soviet intervention in Afghanistan, led to a positive change in the Japanese view of its own role in international security. In 1976 the Japanese government decided to work out with the U.S. government "guidelines for Japan-U.S. defense cooperation" which were completed two years later. The guidelines provided the basis for subsequent studies by the two nations of military scenarios such as a Soviet attack on Hokkaido, another Korean conflict, and the defense of sea lanes. In 1980 Japan decided to participate in RIMPAC (Rim of the Pacific) exercises, together with the United States, Canada, Australia, and New Zealand.

In 1980 the trilateral nations took further steps in pursuing consonant policies. On the subject of economic sanctions against Iran, Foreign Minister Okita visited Luxembourg in April to consult with his EC counterparts. Japan and the EC took joint measures against Moscow in protest of Soviet aggression in Afghanistan, when they met for the Venice Summit in June 1980. It is in that year that Japan began to emphasize "Japan as a member of the Western camp." When the Geneva talks on INF missiles started in November 1981, Japan became concerned that the two superpowers might reach agreement on the reduction of INF deployment in Europe at the expense of Asia. There was speculation that those mobile SS-20 launchers removed from Europe would be transferred to the Soviet Far East. Foreign Minister Abe visited major European capitals in January 1983, and subministerial-level consultations on INF issues also occurred in Tokyo with Britain, France, and West Germany the same year. At the Williamsburg Summit in May 1983, Prime Minister Nakasone signed a joint statement declaring that "the security of our countries is indivisible and must be approached on a global basis."

Looking back over the past 40 years, one can see that the evolution of trilateral consensus on many international issues, particularly the security issues of East Asia, has been remarkable. From this brief review of the change from dissonant to consonant trends in trilateral interests in East Asia, several lessons can be learned that suggest how present and future trilateral interests and involvement should be coordinated and fulfilled. These lessons will be discussed in the final chapter.

III. CURRENT TRILATERAL INVOLVEMENTS AND PERCEPTIONS

How do the trilateral nations perceive the security situations of East Asia and relate their respective national security policies to them? Although their interests are generally consonant, it is useful to discuss what differences do exist in current trilateral perceptions of East Asia and in each country's involvement.

A. EAST ASIA IN THE GLOBAL STRATEGIC BALANCE

1. Soviet Power in Asia

The growing importance of East Asia for the United States was already discussed briefly in Chapter I. The global strategic balance is increasingly determined by Soviet deployment of strategic and theater forces in its Far East area and in the Sea of Okhotsk, and by U.S. deployment of strategic submarines and sea- and air-launched cruise missiles. Because of East Asia's strategic importance, the Soviet Union pays close attention to the development of international relations in East Asia, and it is due to Soviet attention that the Americans also watch security conditions in the region. As Secretary of Defense Caspar Weinberger recently said: "While continuing to tilt the conventional and nuclear balance in Europe further in their favor, the Soviets are also increasing and modernizing their already considerable air and ground forces in Northeast Asia."[1] The Soviet forces are reaching parity with their U.S. counterparts in East Asia. Their buildup may be accelerated under the new leader Mikhail Gorbachev, who came in power in March 1985.

The *United States* considers it essential to remain a Pacific power because of its vital security and economic interests. In the center of the vast ocean it has its own strategic territories: Guam, Hawaii, and American Samoa. It is committed to defending Japan, South Korea, the Philippines and Thailand, as well as Australia and New Zealand. More than 30 percent of U.S. trade is conducted with the countries of East

---

[1] *Report of the Secretary of Defense Caspar W. Weinberger to the Congress*, February 1985, p. 15.

Asia, underscoring their importance to the U.S. economy. The United States is now concerned about New Zealand's refusal to accept U.S. nuclear warships at its ports because it fears that such "irresponsible" attitudes might spread to other U.S. allies, particularly Japan, which supports the indispensable "forward basing" of U.S. forces in the Western Pacific. The United States is also concerned about the naval air logistics and operations base that the Soviets have established at Cam Ranh Bay, Vietnam. It continues to urge Japan to strengthen its defense capability faster and to equip itself with the capability to defend 1,000 miles of sea lanes from its shore and to close off the three international straits along the Japanese islands in wartime. Canada, Western Europe, and Japan essentially share the United States view, yet their opinions of what is most important seem to differ.

Canada, being located between the two superpowers, fears that it "could be exposed to the direct effects on the Canadian population and territory of thermonuclear exchanges between the United States and the Soviet Union."[2] The Soviet Union's buildup of sea-based strategic forces (SLBM) in the Northwest Pacific can endanger Canadian security. SS-20 missiles recently introduced in the Soviet Far East can reach Canada. However, the Canadians do not seem to be as apprehensive about the SLBM and SS-20s as the Americans are. Canada does not perceive itself to be a target of Soviet strategic weapons. The Soviet conventional buildup also seems to be of less concern to Canada. Traditionally the Canadians have viewed themselves as a security link between the North American and West European continents through the North Atlantic Treaty Organization. However, Canada has not reinforced its Pacific defense. Nor does it seem to be as concerned about the Soviet military presence in Indochina as the Americans are, because Canada's primary security concern in the Pacific is maintenance of secure lanes of communication in the northern Pacific between itself and Japan, its largest trading partner after the United States. This concern is reflected in its participation in the annual naval exercise, RIMPAC. But Canada sees its security link with Japan only through its ties with the United States.

Japan has taken a growing interest in the Soviet deployment of nuclear forces in East Asia and the Western Pacific and in the developments at the Geneva INF talks in 1981-83. Japan feels that the United States is losing its position of superiority over Soviet military power in East Asia and the Pacific. But it thinks that the Soviet nuclear threat to its shores is less than the United States does. Japan adheres to its policy

---

[2]Canadian Parliament, Senate, Standing Committee on Foreign Affairs, Subcommittee on National Defense, *Manpower in Canada's Armed Forces*, January 1982.

against nuclear deployment, which denies U.S. nuclear-armed ships access to its ports. Its response to the fast-growing Soviet conventional forces in Asia is slow, and this disturbs the United States. This discrepancy in assessment of the security situation between the two Pacific powers is often a source of friction in their bilateral security relations. Japan tends to emphasize Soviet political, economic and ideological weakness in the Pacific and has been concerned that war may result not just from Soviet aggression but from heightened tension arising from superpower competition.

Western Europe seems to be ambivalent about Soviet nuclear and conventional forces in East Asia. On one hand, the Soviet Union's shift in emphasis toward the Asia-Pacific region may take some pressure off Europe. If future arms control talks between the superpowers on Euromissiles should culminate in the reduction of SS-20 missiles in the European theater and their removal to east of the Urals, West European security would be increased. (At one point the Soviet Union did state that it might move some SS-20 missiles from Europe to Asia.) On the other hand, Western European nations would be discouraged if such a transfer led to a shift in U.S. attention from Europe to Asia. They would also be concerned about the Soviet ability to disrupt sea lanes in the Pacific and Indian Oceans that would affect their highly important trading activities with Japan and other East Asian countries. Major Western European leaders agreed at the 1983 Williamsburg Summit that control of INF missiles should be handled on a global, not regional scale. For the benefit of both Western Europe and Japan, both should take a strong stand on the SS-20 missiles lest the Soviet Union play off its two fronts against each other.

2. Chinese Power

In the context of the global balance, the trilateral countries share the strategic view that a strong PRC counterbalancing Soviet military power is in their favor. However, they seem to differ on the question of how strong the PRC should be.

None of the trilateral countries is sure of whether they should consider China a global power or a regional power. Nor are they certain whether they should or should not treat China as a partner. Although views within each country differ, generally the Americans tend to treat China as both a global power and a strategic partner, and the Canadians and Europeans tend to perceive China as a regional power more capable than Japan of being a credible deterrent to the Soviet Union. For many Europeans, especially the French, concerned about Soviet power, China is practically a 17th member of NATO. China possesses a large, though poorly equipped, army and strategic nuclear arms. What matters is that China is willing to use force. For the Europeans, China is a direct strategic value, because Moscow is more worried about China than about Japan.

For Japan, a friendly and secure China helps prevent the spread of Soviet influence in East Asia. Thus Japan, together with the other trilateral countries, has a strategic interest in strengthening China's political and economic stability. However, the Japanese might have more reservations about too strong a China even though such a China might still be acceptable to Western Europe and Canada. Japan, in this sense, is somewhat disturbed by the emerging Sino-American military cooperation, while Western Europe supports it and is trying to compete with the United States for arms sales. Among Western Europeans perhaps the Germans are the most cautious in approaching the PRC for fear of provoking Moscow.

The United States is more concerned about possible improvement in Sino-Soviet relations, which might unfavorably affect the global strategic balance, than Western Europe is. Western Europeans and perhaps Canadians as well might also be concerned about it to the extent that Soviet attention may be shifted from Asia to Europe and the Middle East. Japan would presumably welcome reduced Sino-Soviet tensions. This tension has caused Soviet military growth in the Far East and inhibited solutions in Korea and Kampuchea.

B. REGIONAL SECURITY

The importance given to East Asia's regional security likewise varies among the trilateral countries. Naturally the United States, being a superpower concerned with its sphere of influence, has a stake in practically all regional issues because they are related to regional security. Other than Japan, which it considers its most stable and reliable security partner in East Asia, the United States is particularly interested in the Korean peninsula and Southeast Asia, because it has security commitments to South Korea, the Philippines, and Thailand. It is also aware of the strategic importance of Singapore and Indonesia. All of these countries have different kinds of problems, but one common denominator is fragility of political institutions, especially mechanisms for leadership succession. For the moment, the United States is the most concerned about the instability of and potential turmoil in the Philippines. Over the past four decades, however, American involvement in East Asia has fluctuated between interventionist and isolationist postures. This has tended to create a credibility gap between the United States and its allies.

Most Western European nations see the issues affecting regional security in East Asia primarily in terms of how each issue affects the U.S. position in maintaining the regional and global balance of power rather than in terms of how they themselves can contribute to that balance. Naturally Canada and the Western European nations are concerned about the progress of East Asia's democratic nations and about basic human needs, but they tend to view the region primarily in economic terms, leaving political leadership to the Americans. Some Western European nations, however, do retain residual political and security interests. At present Britain keeps approximately 9,000 troops in Hong Kong. Britain also maintains one Gurkha infantry battalion and one Royal Marine company plus some military advisors in Brunei, all paid for by the host country which gained complete independence in January 1984. Britain is a party to the Five-Power Defense Arrangement (FPDA) of 1971 under which it is obliged to "consult" with other parties concerning the defense of Singapore and Malaysia, two of its Commonwealth partners. It stations no troops in these countries, but it participates in FPDA joint maneuvers, sells arms, and trains local officers. It is also a party to the Manila Pact of 1954 under which it has a collective security commitment to the Philippines and Thailand. While the United States sees the pact as the basis for the defense of Thailand, Britain seems to behave as if the pact no longer exists. The British do not see themselves participating in armed conflicts in the region.

Ever since it left Indochina in 1954, France has demonstrated no military interest in the region, other than to sell arms (see Table 5). It withdrew from the Manila Pact in November 1973. It still has a political interest in Indochina, for it has kept close contacts with many French-speaking Indochinese leaders, left and right, who have come to Paris as political refugees, exiles, clandestine operators, and the like. France claims to have special cultural relations with the Indochinese countries. President Mitterrand visited Chinese and Kampuchean resistance leaders. In recent months the French have been forced to take greater interest in East Asia and the Pacific because of disputes over independence for New Caledonia, where they have some 2,800 troops and plans to build a large military base in the future.

The Dutch are naturally interested in Indonesia because of their previous colonial connections. They no longer have any intention of interfering politically or militarily as they once did over the Sumatra-Sulawesi rebellion in 1957-1958 and the West Irian (now Irian Jaya) territorial dispute of 1961-1962. After the British administration of Hong Kong ends in 1997, Portugal will be the last colonial country in East Asia; it holds the tiny but active tourist and gambling haven of Macao.

Western Europe pays only limited attention to the Korean peninsula, although Japan and the United States consider it vital to their national security and also claim that their contribution to the security of South Korea is a contribution to the security of Europe, for a secure South Korea allows the United States to pay more attention to Europe. It should be noted that several trilateral nations such as the United States, Britain, and Canada are still engaged in the Military Armistice Commission as part of the U.N. Command. This is also true in a different way of Sweden and Switzerland who are members of the Neutral Nations Supervisory Commission.

Like the European nations, Canada appears to perceive the regional balance of power in East Asia from a smaller power's perspective. It realizes that its role is limited. Traditionally its political contact has been through the Commonwealth. As it looks more toward East Asia, it seeks closer political cooperation with Japan. Under the new Mulroney government elected in September 1984, Canada may adopt a more

TABLE 5

Incidence of Trilateral Countries' Arms Sales to East Asia
(arms sale agreements reached betweeen 1980 and 1984)

	U.S.	CANADA	BELGIUM	DENMARK	FRANCE	WEST GERMANY	IRELAND	ITALY	NETHERLANDS	NORWAY	PORTUGAL	SPAIN	U.K.	SWEDEN	SWITZERLAND
Brunei	x												x		
Burma[1]				x			x								x
China	x				x		x[2]								
Indonesia	x				x	x			x	x		x	x		x
Japan	x												x		
ROK	x					x							x		
Malaysia	x	x			x	x	x					x	x	x	x
Philippines	x														
Singapore	x	x			x				x				x		
Taiwan	x									x					
Thailand	x				x	x			x	x		x	x		

Notes: (1) Agreements reached in 1979.
     (2) Agreements signed in April 1985.
Source: Produced on the basis of data on arms agreement presented in the International Institute for Strategic Studies' *Military Balance* 1980-81 through 1984-85 and the Stockholm International Peace Research Institute's *SIPRI Yearbook 1984* and *SIPRI Yearbook 1985.*

assertive outward-looking foreign and security posture in the future, as it re-emphasizes closer ties with the United States and the need to review its relative place in the world. To Canada, its traditional contribution as a participant in international peace-keeping forces is important—it was so involved after each of the two Indochinese wars. Due to its frustrating experiences in Vietnam, however, it is not likely to serve on any U.N. peace-keeping force in Kampuchea.

Japan, being geographically a part of East Asia, is directly affected by the security environment of the region. But it has chosen not to use force for diplomatic gain. Instead, with its diplomatic and economic activities an integral part of what it terms "a comprehensive national security policy," it claims to be playing an important role in maintaining the regional balance in favor of the non-Communist side. Japan claims its economic aid to China, South Korea, and ASEAN nations helps strengthen these countries vis-a-vis their respective adversaries—the Soviet Union, North Korea, and Vietnam. As Table 6 shows, Japan's annual average official development aid (ODA) for East Asia was $851.8 million in 1977-1982, which was much larger than the combined U.S., Canadian, and European ODA to the same region ($678.5 million). Japan's trilateral partners do not seem to appreciate this. Only in recent years has the United States begun to show its appreciation publicly. But Western Europe and Canada are not convinced by Japan's

TABLE 6

Trilateral Countries' ODA to East Asian Countries
(average annual flow in 1977-82)

(in million U.S. dollars)

	JAPAN	U.S.	CANADA	WESTERN EUROPE*
Burma	114.1	3.0	3.6	55.8
PRC	67.2	—	0.8	20.8
Indonesia	257.9	119.5	16.2	223.2
ROK	96.7	25.7	0.1	21.3
Malaysia	59.6	1.7	1.6	18.1
Philippines	104.5	61.0	1.3	36.1
Singapore	6.0	—	0.2	3.2
Taiwan	−5.9	−8.3	—	3.6
Thailand	151.7	13.5	4.8	52.0
Total	851.8	216.0	28.5	434.0

*Western Europe includes Austria, Belgium, Denmark, Finland, France, West Germany, Italy, Netherlands, Norway, Sweden, Switzerland, and the U.K.

Source: Produced on the basis of figures presented in the OECD's *Geographical Distribution of Financial Flows to Developing Countries.*

argument in favor of its limited military capability and domestic political constraints on a fast defense buildup.

C. THE ECONOMIC POTENTIAL: "THE PACIFIC BASIN"

As more attention is given to the bright economic side of the East Asian region, it is becoming more frequently referred to as part of the broader Asia-Pacific region or the Pacific basin region, which is commonly understood to include the United States, Canada, and Oceania as well as East Asia. Perceptions of the economic potential of the Asia-Pacific region vary among the trilateral nations. The United States, Canada, and Japan are important parts of the Pacific basin and look forward to the future dynamic development of the region whereas Western Europe fears being left out. The United States, Canada, and Japan as well as several smaller nations of the Pacific rim have organized semi-official national committees for Pacific economic cooperation. Of the European nations, France has been most active in seeking acknowledgement as a "Pacific" nation. In 1984 a French institute organized a high-powered seminar under the telling theme: "The Challenge of the Pacific: Western Hopes and Fears?"

Western Europe, North America, and Japan are all competing for economic contacts with the countries in the region, particularly with China, South Korea, and the ASEAN nations. None of them, however, seriously considers the Soviet Far East to be a viable economic actor in the region. All the trilateral nations hold mixed views of China's economic future, but on the whole they are optimistic, speculating that the pragmatic policies of Deng Xiaoping and Hu Yaobang will continue. Most of the top trilateral leaders have visited China in the last few years primarily to promote trade and political relations, and have exchanged views on strategic and other political issues such as the SS-20, Korea, Indochina, Afghanistan and Hong Kong. Japan and the United States are cautious in their dealings with Taiwan, whereas some European nations seem to be less sensitive to the Taiwan issue, as shown in the case of the Dutch sale in 1981 of a submarine to Taiwan, resulting in a temporary rupture of diplomatic relations between the Netherlands and China.

European economic ties with China are, nevertheless, handicapped by geographical and cultural distance. Japan enjoys the advantage of being geographically close to China. Some Europeans speculate on the potential for "Asian" rather than "Pacific" domination in the future—for example, a British novel, *The Third World War* (1978), posits a new "coprosperity sphere" combining Japanese technology and industrial efficiency with the world's largest population in China. Japan and China did establish a bilateral Committee for the 21st Century to promote closer relations as a long-term goal. But few Japanese have any vision of a new Sino-Japanese "coprosperity sphere," pointing to the many uncertainties surrounding China's political and economic future as well as Japan's much more substantial links to its trilateral partners.

Western Europe's trade with ASEAN is growing in terms of volume but not percentage. A little over just one percent of the total of EC trade is with ASEAN, although this represents some 10 to 12 percent of ASEAN's total trade (see Appendix Tables II-1d and II-1e). Britain and West Germany are the two strongest European traders in Southeast Asia, and are ASEAN's third and fourth largest trading partners. Similarly, Canada's trade with ASEAN is not particularly important to Canada. All three countries are easily outranked by Japan and the United States, which are either the first or second biggest traders for most ASEAN nations. In 1983, 66 percent of Indonesia's exports and 56 percent of the Philippines' exports went to Japan and the United States.

TABLE 7

China's Trade⁽¹⁾ with the Trilateral Countries
(in million U.S. dollars)

	1973	1978	1983
Japan	1,949 (17.8%)	4,824 (23.4%)	9,077 (22.3%)
Western Europe⁽²⁾	2,587 (23.6%)	4,125 (20.0%)	6,837 (16.8%)
EC	2,169 (19.8%)	3,294 (16.0%)	5,695 (14.0%)
U.S.	260 (2.4%)	992 (4.8%)	4,024 (9.9%)
Canada	447 (4.1%)	669 (3.2%)	1,527 (3.7%)
World	10,976 (100%)	20,638 (100%)	40,727 (100%)

(1) Exports plus imports.
(2) Western Europe is composed of Austria, Belgium, Britain, Denmark, Finland, France, West Germany, Greece, Iceland, Ireland, Italy, Liechtenstein, Luxembourg, Malta, Monaco, Netherlands, Norway, Portugal, Spain, Sweden, and Switzerland.

Source: Produced on the basis of figures presented in *The Almanac of China's Foreign Economic Relations and Trade* (1984).

Because of its apprehension about being regarded as economically dominating Southeast Asia, Japan welcomes other countries, particularly EC countries, into the region to balance its position. ASEAN also welcomes economic ties with EC countries for the same reason. The EC, the United States, and Canada have bilateral mechanisms of consultation with ASEAN, as does Japan. Britain continues to be a big investor in Hong Kong. But countries like Malaysia and Singapore, with which Britain had traditional economic links, are increasingly "looking East" to learn the techniques of industrial efficiency and the "work ethic" of Japan.

Because of the need to expand their East Asian market, some European countries eye business possibilities in Vietnam and North Korea. Sweden has been a major Western supplier of capital and technology to Vietnam, especially while the Western sanctions against Vietnam were in force, although Swedish aid is very small in comparison to Soviet aid. West Germany has in the past attempted to invest in North Korea through Hong Kong, while France went directly into North Korea in 1984 via a joint venture to construct a large hotel/office building. Japanese businessmen also are eager to enter those socialist economies but are discouraged by North Korea's foreign debts and by their own government's concern about the negative reactions of its more important economic partners such as the ASEAN countries and South Korea.

Despite their large unfavorable trade imbalances with Japan, Japan's trilateral partners see Japan as their most important trading partner in East Asia. In 1982 the EC exported $15.0 billion to East Asia, of which Japan accounted for $6.2 billion. Canada's exports to Japan amounted to $3.7 billion, which was 63 percent of its total exports to East Asia. The United States exported $20.4 billion to Japan, or 50 percent of its exports to East Asia (see Appendix Table II-1a). Canada is paying greater attention to the Japanese market and capital by promoting an economic triangle relationship between the west coast of Canada, the west coast of the United States, and Japan. Western Europe appears challenged and threatened by the close economic interdependence between the United States and Japan, particularly by their technological cooperation, which, it fears, may ultimately benefit the development of the NICs and ASEAN more than itself.

Thus, with varying and often dissonant perceptions of East Asia's position in the global balance and in the international economy as well as their own security in the region, the trilateral nations share the common assessment that greater importance has to be attached to the region.

IV. NEW STRATEGIC SITUATIONS IN EAST ASIA

As the year 1985 opened, the four big powers on both sides of the Pacific were making new attempts to assert their national interests and were trying to tip the strategic balance in their respective favors. Moscow and Washington were trying to impress each other and the publics of their allies with their sincerity by talking about arms reduction. In the last days of 1984, the Soviet Union and China signed economic agreements, making their relationship more normalized. In January 1985 the top American military leaders visited Beijing to discuss security cooperation with the Chinese leaders. In the same month Prime Minister Nakasone visited the United States and Oceania to demonstrate that a trans-Pacific partnership exists among the industrialized democracies.

At that very time New Zealand and the United States began to experience tension over the former's refusal to allow U.S. nuclear warships to dock at its ports. The United States expressed concern about the future of ANZUS. North Korea once again condemned the planned U.S.-South Korean joint military maneuvers, called Team Spirit '85, and attributed its refusal to have ministerial talks with its southern adversary to the fact that these maneuvers took place. Since the completion of the military exercise, the two sides have begun to talk to each other. Meanwhile South Korea is expanding economic contacts with China in an apparent attempt to lay the groundwork for further political communications. In Southeast Asia, the Sino-Vietnamese border was becoming tense again, as Vietnamese-led forces eliminated resistance bases in the western border region of Kampuchea.

Where are these developments likely to lead? How might they affect the security of the trilateral countries and their other interests? Here it will be useful to evaluate the implications of Soviet and Chinese objectives and their achievements for the security of the non-Communist countries of East Asia and the responses by the United States and Japan.

A. ASSESSING SOVIET POLITICO-MILITARY ACHIEVEMENTS

1. Soviet Force Buildup in East Asia and the Pacific

The impressive military deployments by the Soviet Union in East Asia and the Pacific and its diplomatic activities suggest that the Soviet Union wishes to acquire the status of a full-fledged Asia-Pacific power, competing with its principal rival, the United States. Through a fast force buildup in its Far East naval bases Moscow wants to strengthen its defense of its thinly populated Far Eastern areas, to increase its capacity to project its power into the Pacific and the Indian Oceans, and to intimidate its East Asian adversaries. To gain the status of an Asia-Pacific power, it employs both military and non-military tactics, using a mixture of compromising and high-handed approaches, depending upon the opportunities available.

In the military field, the Soviet Union now deploys one-quarter to one-third of its entire military capabilities, nuclear and conventional, in its Asia-Pacific areas. According to U.S. and Japanese sources, modernized strategic land- and air-launched missiles (SS-18s and Back-fires) are deployed along the trans-Siberian railroad, and submarine-launched ballistic missiles (SLBMs) are in the Sea of Okhotsk. The number of intermediate-range nuclear forces (INF) is rapidly increasing; some 135 SS-20 missiles are located in Siberia and the area east of Lake Baikal, along with 80 long-range Backfire bombers. Of the Soviet Union's total of 194 army divisions, about 40 divisions (370,000 troops) are supposed to be deployed east of Lake Baikal. The modern MiG-23, MiG-27, and SU-24 comprise over 70 percent of the Soviet fighters in the Far East, and the total number of operational planes is some 2,220. Finally, the Pacific Fleet, composed of about 825 ships, is larger than the other three Soviet fleets. The Pacific Fleet includes 90 major surface combatants and 135 submarines, of which some 65 are nuclear powered, and is primarily based at Vladivostok and Petropavlovsk. Two of the Soviet Union's three aircraft carriers are in the Pacific.

These Soviet deployments are impressive and certainly have enhanced Soviet capabilities in several ways, but they require a balanced analysis. First, alarmists argue that the Sea of Okhotsk is becoming a "sanctuary" for Soviet strategic submarine forces because they can be reserved as secure second-strike forces against the Americans. However, the U.S. contests the notion that the Sea of Okhotsk and the Sea of Japan are becoming "Soviet lakes." Task forces from the U.S. Seventh Fleet often enter these seas for naval maneuvers, demonstrating the U.S. right to be there.

Second, although the Soviet Union deploys a larger number of submarines in the Pacific than the United States does, the quality of those submarines is inferior to that of their American counterparts. This is equally true of the quality of Soviet carriers. They are essentially helicopter carriers; they do not sail as much in peacetime as the U.S. carriers do either. Soviet ships are often seen being towed because of mechanical breakdown. Above all, what should be noted is that unlike its American rival, the Soviet navy has not participated in combat in the postwar years.

Third, impressive as the quantity of Soviet military power may be, the KAL incident of September 1983 revealed that its air defense system leaves much to be desired. Although the Soviet Union has some 40 divisions in the Far East, only 35 percent of them are at a 75 percent to 100 percent level of combat readiness. The Soviets may pose a threat to Chinese security, but with only two *Rogov*-class amphibious ships, each of which can carry about 40 tanks and 800 troops, and a naval Special Force (Spetsnaz Marines) brigade attached to the Pacific Fleet, there is a serious limit to their ability to project military force across the seas.

This situation notwithstanding, the pace of Soviet force buildup in the region is still impressive. This suggests that the non-Communist countries of the region should watch Soviet deployment with great care and take, individually and collectively, measures necessary to cope with it—for, under Gorbachev, Moscow may become more assertive in expanding its sphere of influence to weaken the United States.

2. The Soviet Military Presence in Indochina

One of the great strategic benefits that the Russians gained from the American defeat in Vietnam was a closer security tie with Vietnam. In Danang and Cam Rahn Bay, the Soviets now have about 10 medium-range bombers (Badgers), and 20 to 25 warships, plus an electronic monitoring station. An official American source claims that there also are MiG-23 fighters. Approximately 2,500 Russian military personnel are stationed there. One source even claims there are 7,000 to 8,000 military advisors and technicians there as well. These facilities in Vietnam have given Moscow the capability to project its power over the region and into the Indian Ocean. This capability could become even more effective if the Soviets should also attain an equivalent position in Afghanistan. Soviet air and naval forces can threaten the Western Pacific sea lanes and U.S. bases in the Philippines. In the Sino-Vietnamese war in early 1979 Soviet planes flew over the South China Sea in a possible threat to nullify Chinese claims to the islands in these areas. In April 1984 Soviet naval forces practiced landing near Haiphong, presumably to demonstrate to the Chinese their ability to assist the Vietnamese in a future Hanoi-Beijing conflict.

The Soviet use of bases in Vietnam as well as in South Yemen and Ethiopia is certainly unique to its Pacific Fleet. No other Soviet fleet has access to overseas facilities in the same fashion. Such a military presence can certainly intimidate the nations of the Pacific, and perhaps those of the Indian Ocean rim as well during peacetime. However, during wartime, especially in a prolonged international conflict, the Soviets would have difficulty in retaining logistical support for those overseas facilities because their sea lane between Vladivostok and Cam Rahn Bay could be easily cut. What is more, there is reason to believe that the Soviet Union has some serious friction with the xenophobic Vietnamese, despite and perhaps because of the latter's growing dependence on Russia for its national survival. Ninety-seven percent of Vietnamese arms are Soviet-supplied. Moscow also wants to have direct contact with Laos and Kampuchea. There are approximately 500 Russian military advisors in Laos, and the Soviet engineers and other specialists in Kampuchea have enlarged and modernized the port of Kompong Som (old Sihanoukville) and built an air field large enough to accommodate the MiG-23. Vietnamese personnel are reportedly kept away from some of these facilities. Hanoi probably is not happy with such Soviet activities. Hanoi-Moscow relations may become cool in the future, particularly if Sino-Soviet relations continue to improve. Such relations could limit the latter's use of facilities in Vietnam at a critical moment.

3. Limited Soviet Political Presence in East Asia

Moscow's diplomatic achievements in the region are remarkably few. In 1969 Brezhnev tried to seize an opportunity to increase the Soviet influence over East Asia when the United States was struggling to end the unpopular Vietnam war. None of the East Asian countries responded positively to his proposal for an Asian collective security system. Instead, in 1971 the ASEAN nations proposed a zone of peace, freedom and neutrality (ZOPFAN) for the region. Only in 1978 did Vietnam sign a bilateral security treaty with the Russians. Moscow's relations with Tokyo are strained to the point that there is no prospect for early improvement, while its relations with Beijing have improved but have limits, as will be discussed later. The Soviet Union has only four allies in East Asia—North Korea, Vietnam, Laos, and the Vietnam-backed Heng Samrin government of Kampuchea—all of which suffer from weak, unsuccessful economies and are eager to obtain Western goods and capital.

Russia's own stagnant economy attracts none of the countries in the region oriented toward a market economy. But the Soviet Union has sought political influence by offering a nuclear power plant to the Philippines, by buying up a sizeable quantity of natural rubber from Malaysia, and by intimidating the Japanese with its force buildup. Its primary objective seems to be to weaken U.S. influence in the region. For this reason, practically all countries that are concerned about Soviet military power and that approve of the U.S. counterbalance are its targets: China, Japan, and South Korea in Northeast Asia, and the six ASEAN countries. Current Soviet diplomacy appears to be aimed at the Philippines because of its political turmoil, active Communist subversives, and the large U.S. bases which in a crisis could isolate the Soviet military presence in Vietnam. The Soviets also are courting Jakarta with the aim of causing a rift between those ASEAN countries which favor political compromise with Hanoi over the Kampuchean issue and hard-liners like Thailand. The Soviet Union may also want to forestall any rapprochement between Indonesia and China.

These Soviet tactics are not likely to work. If the Soviets increase their diplomatic activities in Asia in an attempt to generate fear of China or fear of "the revival of Japanese militarism," they will not gain the support of Southeast Asian leaders, who would claim that they know how to manage their problems with China and that Japanese military capability can in no way lead to militarism under the present circumstances.

B. ASSESSING A "NEW CHINA"

The pragmatic leadership in China, headed by Deng Xiaoping, Hu Yaobang and Zhao Ziyang, will be instrumental in bringing about another "new China." There have been so many "new Chinas," and even under Deng's leadership there was one "new China" prior to the 12th Party Congress in 1982 and one after that. There is naturally some continuity in the past two phases of the Deng-Hu-Zhao leadership, but one distinctive difference is the pro-U.S. stand taken before 1982 and the "independent" stand taken after that year. This changed foreign policy emphasis affects China's relationships with the United States and the Soviet Union and, consequently, the triangular relationship among the three powers, as well as the quadrangular relationship that includes Japan.

Since its foundation in 1949, the People's Republic of China has had a most unpredictable foreign policy. This reflects China's struggle to find a balance between two conflicting forces: ideologues and pragmatists, or the "Reds" and "experts." The current claim for "independence," which is different from the "self-reliance" outcry of the late 1950s and the 1960s, may fit within the pragmatist tradition. The current stand calls for a normalized relationship with the Soviet Union in contrast to the previous anti-Soviet policy, while at the same time continuing friendly relations with the industrialized democracies. Premier Zhao Ziyang's report made to the Second Session of the 6th National People's Congress in May 1984 was telling: "We take a principled stand in handling our relations with the United States and the Soviet Union. We will not refrain from improving relations with them because we oppose their hegemonism, nor will we give up anti-hegemonist stand because we want to improve relations with them, nor will we try to improve our relations with one of them at the expense of the other."[1] Simply put, China now refuses to be a "China card" for either the United States or the Soviet Union. China seems to have learned that its pro-U.S. and anti-Soviet stance of the 1970s narrowed rather than widened its policy options. Its current strategy appears to be (1) to strengthen its own national power through modernization programs, (2) to seek closer contacts with the Third World in order to broaden its diplomatic base in international forums, and (3) to improve relations with both the United States and the Soviet Union in order to exploit maximum political and economic resources from both.

Yet the reality of China's foreign relations is far from its claim of independence. Certainly, its relations with Moscow have improved, but it has much closer relations with the trilateral countries than it does with the Soviet Union. The current economic reform will be a key to the success of the "four modernization programs"; China wishes to quadruple industrial production by the year 2000. Its economic reform policies are far ranging. Its four "special economic zones" plus 14 more coastal cities and Hainan Island are to become industrial zones on the capitalist model, for they are open to foreign investments. People's communes, which used to be the basis for the Chinese socialist economy, have been replaced by the contract system which encourages the individual entrepreneurial spirit. The prosperity of the rural sector creates political pressure on Communist Party leaders to introduce similar "free entreprise" systems in the urban sector as well. In October 1984 the party decided to reform the economic structure itself. To carry

---

[1] *Beijing Review*, May 21, 1984, p.19.

out this reform, China needs more capital and technology, which the industrialized democracies can offer best.

Practically all the industrial democracies today take a keen interest in increasing economic and political contacts with China. This nicely fits China's strategy to enhance its own international status. Competition among the industrialized democracies for access to the Chinese market gives the advantage to the Chinese, who can certainly exploit such competition. The question is whether the industrialized democracies think that the benefits of doing business in China outweigh the losses mutual competition implies, and how long they can wait before getting some return on their investment. In other words, can China remain attractive as a market for foreign investors long enough for it to make use of external economic relations to catch up with the international free market system? While China cannot produce goods which are competitive in the markets of the industrialized democracies, it has to develop export markets in order to gain the hard currency it needs for imports from the industrialized democracies. This need for new export markets may reinforce China's current call for solidarity with the Third World to a significant extent, but it may be regarded increasingly as a competitor by developing Asian countries. Naturally, Hong Kong will continue to be a good source of hard currency for China.

The smooth negotiations concluded between China and Britain over the reversion in 1997 of Hong Kong have contributed greatly to bringing about a measure of peaceful transition. China's stated policy for "one nation, two systems" seems to reinforce the climate for it. But there are many uncertain factors that could easily destroy the climate. A main problem may be that foreign capital and Hong Kong Chinese capital at present already invested in Hong Kong will not stay and a new flow of investments will not be forthcoming, depending upon how China treats Hong Kong between now and 1997. Hong Kong's capitalist system (GNP was $26 billion in 1982 with an average annual growth rate of 9.6 percent for 1978-82) may exert a greater impact on the Mainland's special economic districts along the coast than China expects it will. Hong Kong businessmen boast of "capitalizing all of China." Such situations would invite China to tighten its control over Hong Kong, whereas the population of Hong Kong, which now exceeds 5.3 million, certainly needs continued economic growth. The situation could deteriorate further if people in Hong Kong start leaving. Where can they go? And who will take them? Taiwan is already sending discouraging signals because it fears Chinese agents may try to sneak in.

How long China's current transformation will last and how far it will go remains to be seen. What happens depends more on domestic power relations between "experts" and "Reds" than on the international environment. There are already some signs that the Chinese economy is expanding too quickly. In 1984 the growth rate for agricultural and industrial production was about 14 percent, which alarmed the Chinese leaders. The encouragement of individual incentives also has led to extensive speculation, growth of the lottery, and graft in some quarters. Economic mismanagement will create political tensions, which would discourage the inflow of foreign capital. The demise of Deng Xiaoping may culminate in such an intense power struggle within the Party that "capitalist" reformists find themselves deadlocked. The People's Liberation Army and the old Red Guards are not entirely happy with the pragmatic approach to national development. The new China's future is not altogether bright.

C. NEW INTERACTIONS AMONG THE GREAT POWERS

1. Sino-Soviet Relations

The current gradual improvement of relations between the Soviet Union and China, which began in about 1981 and became more noticeable after 1982, stems more from the latter's shift in policy than from the former's. China's initial response to Brezhnev's Tashkent speech of March 1981, in which the Soviet leader called for improved bilateral relations, was harsh. China was adamant about the "three conditions for normalization"—Soviet troop withdrawal from Mongolia, troop withdrawal from Afghanistan, and Soviet withdrawal of support for Vietnam's military occupation of Kampuchea—proposed in 1979. Yet the Chinese obviously saw the benefit of improving state-to-state relations with the Russians, even without the three conditions being fulfilled. Along with the border demarcation talks, the Chinese have agreed to move toward closer trade and cultural relations. A significant event took place in late 1984, when First Deputy Premier Ivan Arkhipov, who in May of that year had abruptly cancelled a scheduled visit to China, did visit and signed three agreements on long-term economic, technical and scientific cooperation. These were the first agreements of their kind since the Russian specialists left China in 1960 and the bilateral security treaty of 1950 became invalid in April 1980.

Trade between the two countries tripled between 1982 and 1983, and increased by 70 percent between 1983 and 1984. Border trade is also active, as passenger and freight train service has been resumed along the border. The Soviets have also expressed interest in participating in joint ventures and extending cooperation in the development of the northwestern region of China. The two countries also began to accept exchange students.

Yet there is no sign that the Soviet Union is likely to meet any one of China's three conditions for normalization. China seems to find the Soviet Union vulnerable to China's demands regarding these conditions. It can use them as a useful political weapon or bargaining chip against Russia, when that suits its interests, as China uses the Taiwan issue in its dealings with the United States. In November 1984 China was reported to have declined to discuss Soviet-proposed confidence-building measures (CBM)—namely, giving advance mutual notification of those military maneuvers that will take place on both sides of the common border—because such a proposal reflects the Soviet intention not to disengage any of its forces from the border. China also criticizes the Soviet Union's incremental deployment of SS-20 missiles east of the Urals. China seems determined to modernize the People's Liberation Army with its own and Western technology, refusing to have any association with the Soviet military. There are no mutual visits of military officials between Moscow and Beijing, nor have there yet been visits of top party officials. There is still a clear limit to the Sino-Soviet reconciliation, a limit that suggests that current moves for limited reconciliation represent little more than a tactical detente.

2. Sino-American Relations

In mid-1985 the United States and China are on good terms, despite the latter's pronounced assertions of its "independent" foreign policy and criticism of some aspects of U.S. foreign behavior, especially in Central America. For both strategic and economic reasons, the United States is offering various forms of assistance to China, including commercial joint ventures, academic scientific training, technology transfer, and military force modernization. Despite the thorny Taiwan issue of 1981-82 and other problems (such as the defection of a tennis player in 1982) which damaged bilateral relations, a higher level of national interests on both sides effected a move to restore relations after 1983. The Taiwan issue, in particular, is avoided.

In the technology transfer area, the United States decided in June 1983 to treat China as "a non-aligned, friendly country" and to allow the transfer of sophisticated dual-use technology to it. Between early 1983 and early 1985 both governments exchanged visits by many high-ranking leaders, including Secretary of State George Shultz, Secretary

of Commerce Malcolm Baldridge, Secretary of Defense Caspar Weinberger, Foreign Minister Wu Xueqian, Premier Zhao Ziyang, President
Ronald Reagan, Defense Minister Zhang Aiping, Secretary of the Navy
John F. Lehman, Jr., Chairman of the the Joint Chiefs of Staff General
John Vessey, Jr., and Commander-in-Chief of U.S. Forces Pacific Admiral William Crowe. It is remarkable that U.S. military-related officials
visiting Beijing tend to be of higher rank than their Chinese counterparts visiting Washington. The Americans go to Beijing to discuss
strategic relations between their country and China, while the Chinese
come to Washington to consult on the purchase of U.S. arms. The
United States has agreed to transfer anti-tank missiles (TOW) and anti-
aircraft missiles useful for China's border defense. In January 1985
General Vessey visited the northeast and southern regions of China
and inspected the Sino-Soviet and Sino-Vietnamese borders. It is significant that the highest ranking U.S. military officer has visited these
places.

The U.S. purpose is to demonstrate Sino-American strategic cooperation to Moscow, whereas China's purpose is to modernize its armed
forces by taking advantage of the U.S. willingness to cooperate. This
difference was reflected in the People's Daily's deliberate deletion of the
portion in Reagan's speech made during his stay in Beijing condemning Soviet military behavior. It is in China's interest to exhibit
Sino-American intimacy to the Russians for bargaining purposes and
deterrence but not to increase the level of hostilities with them. The
United States has reportedly warned China that a marked improvement in Sino-Soviet relations could jeopardize the transfer of technology to Beijing. The difference in emphasis notwithstanding, the basic
interests of the United States and China are complementary and close.
A politically close relationship between China and the United States
would also help the U.S. maintain the balance of power in the Korean
peninsula.

There are limits to bilateral military cooperation between the United
States and China, however. First, China will continue to use its strategic position vis-a-vis the superpowers as a bargaining chip in extracting
more military support from the United States. The United States will
find it difficult to respond without compromising on the Taiwan issue.
Second, most ASEAN countries are apprehensive about China becoming stronger militarily and economically and interfering with the region through their support of local Chinese. The United States will be
constrained by its concern not to hurt its relations with ASEAN. Third,
China's limited purchasing capacity will discourage greater and faster
transfer of military hardware.

Taiwan will continue to be a thorny issue between Washington and Beijing, as the latter makes determined gestures to "liberate" Taiwan and incorporate it under its own jurisdiction and the former insists upon a peaceful solution for such incorporation. To the Beijing leaders, the Chinese-British solution of Hong Kong as reached in 1984 would hopefully set a convincing model for Taiwan, but Taipei's reactions to the Hong Kong solution so far have been quite cautious. President Chiang Ching-kuo strongly refuses the idea of "reconciliation." The issue of reintegration is further complicated by the emerging younger leadership generation composed of locally-born Chinese and ethnic Taiwanese who are even less inclined toward Beijing-Taipei rapprochement than Chiang's group. The Taiwan Lobby in the United States constrains Washington's possible moves to abandon Taipei in view of better relations with Beijing.

Both the United States and China today find it in their respective interests to deemphasize the Taiwan issue for more important strategic relations involving Moscow.

3. Soviet-Japanese Relations

Soviet objectives toward Japan are to neutralize it politically, thus undermining the U.S. position in the Western Pacific, and to obtain Japanese capital and technology for the development of Siberia. The Russians employ both heavy-handed and friendly gestures, but they have not been successful. Bilateral relations were at a low point after 1980 and have only very recently improved slightly. In an attempt to sever Japan from American military protection, the Soviets often try to intimidate the Japanese with demonstrations of their force deployments in the Western Pacific. Moscow condemns "the revival of Japanese militarism" so as to encourage those critical of increased Japanese defense efforts to disseminate Soviet displeasure. It further promises not to wage a nuclear attack on Japan so long as Japan adheres to its current policy of prohibiting nuclear deployments on Japanese territories. These actions and policies make obvious Moscow's desire to weaken Japan's security relationship with the United States.

Concerning the thorniest bilateral issue, the Northern Territories, the Soviet Union absolutely refuses even to acknowledge the existence of a territorial dispute. It continues to enlarge and modernize its forces on the islands; it now deploys there some 40 MiG-23s, attack MI-24 helicopters and long-range 130 millimeter cannons. This posture hardens Japan's attitude toward the Soviet Union and justifies even closer security cooperation between Japan and the United States. The Soviets also use fishery issues in the Sea of Okhotsk for political purposes. In early 1984 they successfully demanded the use of a Japanese fishing port in exchange for Japanese fishing quotas. In early 1985 they demanded two ports, including the port of Yokohama, adjacent to the large and sensitive U.S. naval base at Yokosuka, though this demand was naturally rejected. The Soviet Union, in need of capital and technology to develop Siberia, has been trying to lure Japanese investments with little success. Japanese businessmen are less attracted to Siberian energy resources today than they were ten years ago because Japan's industrial structure is well adjusted to the need to save energy. Japanese businessmen are put off further by the poor railroads, ports, and communications system in Siberia. Moscow announced in October 1984 that its 4,200 kilometer BAM (Baikal-Amur Main Line) railroad was completed but admitted that construction was hardly completed enough to allow operation. In 1983 the USSR accounted for only 1.9 percent of Japan's exports and 1.2 percent of its imports. The corresponding percentages in 1975 were 2.9 percent and 2.0 percent. Despite Soviet interest, there is no sign of a long-term economic and trade agreement between the two countries.

Japan and the Soviet Union have the weakest communications links of the four big powers facing the Pacific. It is also the trilateral country with the least interaction with the USSR. The highest-ranking Soviet official who has visited Japan so far is First Deputy Premier Anastas Mikoyan in 1961. Andrei Gromyko's last visit to Japan as Foreign Minister was in 1976. So far only two Japanese prime ministers have been to Moscow officially: Hatoyama in 1956 and Tanaka in 1973. In March 1985 Nakasone had a brief meeting with General Secretary Gorbachev in Moscow on the occasion of Chernenko's funeral, and the meeting produced some hope for a Gromyko visit to Tokyo in late 1985.[2] Yet there is little prospect for close dialogue in the near future.

4. Sino-Japanese Relations

For some time after 1972 when Japan and China normalized their relations, China sought substantial security cooperation with Japan, which was unresponsive. Today, the Chinese leaders seem to understand the domestic political constraints Japan has concerning such cooperation. Still, it is in China's interest to promote friendly relations with Japan in order to gain economic and technical assistance for its modernization programs; and to use Sino-Japanese relations as a diplo-

---

[2]In early July 1985, Eduard A. Shevardnadze was appointed as the new Soviet Foreign Minister, and this is likely to delay the realization of ministerial talks in Tokyo.

matic lever in dealing with the Soviet Union. Japan basically accepts this state of relations, particularly because China has now stopped condemning "Soviet hegemonism."

Japan wants to promote the political stability and economic growth of China so that the latter can effectively resist Soviet influence and become a growing market for Japanese exports, but not to the extent that it appears that Japan and China are united against Soviet hegemonism. This posture encourages various types of contacts between the two countries, ranging from the dispatch of Japanese language teachers and the training of Chinese factory management officials to the construction of infrastructure and a nuclear power plant. In 1983, a total of 188,000 people visited back and forth, although traffic between Japan and Taiwan was much heavier—930,000 people. The trade volume in 1984 was more than $13 billion, making Japan by far China's leading trade partner. Hu Yaobang, Party Secretary in China, came to Tokyo in November 1983, and Prime Minister Nakasone returned his visit in March 1984. The two governments formed a Japan-China Friendship Committee for the 21st Century to make policy recommendations to both governments for promoting a long-term, stable relationship. For National Day in October 1984, Hu Yaobang invited a delegation of 3,000 Japanese youths to visit. Defense Minister Zhang Aiping came to Tokyo for the first time in 1984 to exchange views on international issues and to promote the exchange of defense-related specialists. Haruo Natsume, Vice Minister of the Defense Agency, returned the visit in May 1985 and Koichi Kato, Minister of State, is also planning to go to Beijing for an exchange of views. There is no prospect, however, of arms transfers or joint military exercises between the two countries.

5. Japan-U.S. Relations

Prime Minister Yasuhiro Nakasone, who came into office in November 1982, has changed the Japanese posture toward the United States from one of being a "passive ally" to one of being an "active ally," although his precedessors, Masayoshi Ohira (1978-80) and Zenko Suzuki (1980-82), had to a great extent laid the groundwork for this shift. Nakasone took steps to conclude affirmatively the long-standing legalistic debate over Japanese defense technology transfer to the United States. Within half a year after he took office, he visited South Korea and the ASEAN nations and gained their endorsement of Japan's incremental defense buildup. At the 1984 Williamsburg Summit meeting Nakasone advocated the unity of the Western allies and supported the U.S. deployment of INF missiles in Europe.

What is more important, Nakasone's government revised the former narrow interpretation of the legal perimeter of Self-Defense Force (SDF) cooperation with U.S. forces. The past position confined joint Japan-U.S. naval operations only to Japanese territorial waters. The new position is that it is constitutional for the SDF to assist and defend U.S. warships, including nuclear-armed ones, on the high seas "when Japan is under attack." It will enable Japanese and U.S. forces to operate jointly to defend Japan's sea lanes 1,000 miles from the shore.

The Japanese government still retains a strict policy of prohibiting nuclear deployment, namely, no possession, no manufacture, and no introduction from the outside. There is no significant impact of New Zealand's recent antinuclear decision on the Japanese policy so far. The domestic political climate continues to oppose the production of what may be categorized as "offensive" weapons such as carriers, large-size submarines, and bombers, not to speak of chemical weapons and nuclear arms. The climate also favors the continued existence of the current security policy — namely, the Constitution's denial of the "right of belligerency" and the government's upholding of the "defense only" policy and the security treaty with the United States in which Japan exercises only the right to individual, not collective, self-defense. Thus there are clear limits to Japan's defense capability and its role in international security.

Nonetheless, the domestic political climate is slowly changing to support the government's positive defense posture. A U.S. nuclear-powered carrier, the Carl Vinson, suspected by the mass media of carrying nuclear arms, came to Yokosuka in December 1984, but the size of protest demonstrations was much smaller than expected. After April 1985 the United States started to deploy F-16 fighters at the Misawa air base, and opposition parties raised no serious objections. The Komeito and the Democratic Socialist Party accept the ruling party's defense policy in principle. The new leadership under Chairman Masashi Ishibashi of the Socialist Party, the largest opposition party, is trying to break away from its traditional policy of unarmed neutrality.

The public, furthermore, seems to accept the application of dual-use high technology in the nation's defense, for improving the quality of communication, intelligence, and weapons systems for the SDF. As Japanese technology develops in such fields as semi-conductors, fine ceramics, optical fibers, robotics, lasers, and the like, the country may be able to produce more sophisticated "defense only" weapons. Included among such weapons may be anti-submarine warfare (ASW) devices, stealth fighters, laser beam weapons, electronic countermeasures (ECM), electronic counter-countermeasures (ECCM), precision-guided munitions, and cruise missiles. Some of these are already being deployed. Japan may also develop dual-use space technology in the foreseeable future. Such technology may be used for the U.S. development of the Strategic Defense Initiative (SDI). It is this high technology, competitive with American counterparts, plus Japan's new stance toward positive defense that make Japan-U.S. security relations stronger than before. Japan and the United States, whose leaders have similar views on East Asia and whose combined gross national products comprise 32 percent of the world's GNP, are in a position to be the core for other types of trans-Pacific security cooperation.

A major current hindrance to such security cooperation is the huge trade imbalance, $36.8 billion in favor of Japan in 1984, which has little prospect of being contained. The Japanese tend to blame the Americans for maintaining high interest rates and a strong U.S. dollar and producing less competitive goods. Nakasone's efforts to open up Japan's markets faster have persistently been resisted by domestic industrial and farming groups as well as bureaucrats concerned. The U.S. Congress, annoyed by Japan's slow reactions, is becoming increasingly impatient. There is no guarantee that the economic tensions will not spill over into the security relations or that Nakasone's successors will follow his stance.

D. TRANS-PACIFIC SECURITY COOPERATION

A discussion of the new power interactions in East Asia cannot be complete without referring to the emerging network of security cooperation among those Pacific rim countries which are concerned with the growing Soviet military presence in the Western Pacific. The new security network is not replacing existing treaty arrangements but is using them as a foundation. Two possible triangular partnerships for trans-Pacific cooperation often mentioned are the U.S.-Japan-South Korea and U.S.-Japan-China links. None of the parties to these triangles have referred to themselves as such, but they are condemned as such by the Soviet Union and Vietnam. These are not formal triangular security relationships, and under the present circumstances Japan would certainly find it politically impossible to join such security arrangements. Yet such relationships may actually evolve in the future, or may indeed claim their own de facto existence in an embryonic stage.

A U.S.-Japan-South Korea alliance would logically meet the interests of these parties, but in different degrees. For the U.S. forces, there is no boundary between Japan and South Korea; U.S. forces stationed in Japan have a major mission to defend South Korea as well as Japan. The U.S. Air Force treats Japanese and Korean air space as one and the same. The security of South Korea is among Japan's vital interests, and South Korea needs Japan as the base for logistical support of U.S. operations in the Korean peninsula. But because of Constitutional constraints, Japan can play no military role on the Korean peninsula; nor does South Korea really want it. Bitter memories of Japanese colonialism still prevent South Korea from depending upon Tokyo's protection, despite the fact that Nakasone and Chun Doo Hwan have succeeded to a significant degree in cementing their bilateral relations. Japan's role in South Korea's security is still non-military, providing economic and technological aid and diplomatic support.

Nevertheless, the two countries find it useful to move toward low-level security cooperation as Japan-South Korea relations are gradually improved and as they see the need to exchange military intelligence and to coordinate military operations in order to be able to close off the Tsushima Straits to the Soviets in wartime. Japan is not willing to transfer arms and arms technology to South Korea, but the exchange of military officials has been undertaken on a small scale. In this way, contacts between Japan and South Korea will become more solid, filling in the gap between the two security treaties that the United States has in Northeast Asia. Low-level tripartite consultations may be realized in the not remote future.

A U.S.-Japan-China triangle is also highly unlikely to emerge as a formal structure. Although Japan has changed its outlook on its own role in international security and the three countries tend to share common strategic interests, a de facto triangular security relationship is not foreseen at the moment. As long as Washington treats China as a nonaligned, friendly country, and China claims to hold an independent policy position, the scope and level of mutual security cooperation is limited. There is currently an active two-way flow of military-related people, including cabinet members and arms trade teams, between the two countries, and this may lead to a more institutionalized consultative scheme. Yet neither country has a desire to enter into a formal alliance. The prevailing view in Japan is that it is in the national interest that there be a strong and friendly China, capable of resisting Soviet influence and aggression and thus serving as a positive element in an East Asian balance of power. For these reasons, Japan will provide political and economic support for China, but because China's political and economic future remains uncertain, Japan's aid will be extended cautiously until there is more confidence in China's longer-term orientation. U.S.-Japan-China relations will remain a loose grouping for strategic cooperation—loose but effectively anti-Soviet.

While a U.S.-Japan-China alliance is not feasible, there are other trans-Pacific relations which may begin to assume security dimensions. They relate to possible links among the United States, Canada and Japan; among the United States, Japan, and Australia; among the United States, Japan, and the Philippines; between the United States and ASEAN; between ANZUS and the Five-Power Defense Arrangement (FPDA); and so on. The common denominator here is naturally the United States. Canada and Japan may increase their political links, discussing security issues of mutual concern such as Sino-Soviet relations and the security of North Pacific sea lanes. The Filipinos, who have bitter wartime memories of Japanese occupation, may resist the idea of developing a scheme for security consultation with Japan. But the two countries plus the United States share the interest of keeping the Western Pacific sea lanes open, and this may eventually encourage the three to develop an informal forum for security consultation. The United States and ASEAN will not establish a formal security arrangement, since Indonesia, Malaysia, and Singapore are nonaligned. But on a bilateral basis, the United States has set up defense cooperation such as arms sales, officer training, and joint maneuvers with these countries. The current cold relations between New Zealand and the United States will make it difficult to make ANZUS function as the latter wants it to. Consequently, ANZUS and FPDA cannot expect to set up an early program for consultation and cooperation, but if the United States and New Zealand should successfully adjust themselves to a new working relationship, ANZUS-FPDA coordination seems to be an acceptable multilateral mechanism for trans-Pacific security cooperation.

E. KOREA

The new phases of bilateral relations among the four big powers discussed above could exert great impact on the situations in Korea and Indochina. On the whole, the North-South balance on the Korean peninsula is moving in the South's favor on almost all accounts. This should encourage the North to face reality; but instead it may encourage the North to wage an armed attack before its position becomes even more hopeless. The South has maintained impressive economic viability, with GNP growth at 9.5 percent in 1983 and 7.5 percent in 1984, and per capita income at $1,997 in 1984. This is in contrast to North Korea's much lower 1983 growth rate of 4.3 percent and estimated per capita income of $765. In 1983 the South exported $24.4 billion, while the North exported only $1.4 billion. Diplomatically, Seoul is recognized by 124 countries, and Pyongyang by 103 countries after four countries withdrew recognition because of the Rangoon incident of October 1983. That incident itself may have reflected a growing sense of desperation in some North Korean quarters.

Nakasone's visit to Seoul in January 1983 and President Chun Doo Hwan's historic visit to Tokyo in September 1984 consolidated Japan-South Korea relations, despite numerous grievances about the persistently growing trade imbalances (some $2.6 billion in Japan's favor in 1983). President Reagan's trip to Seoul in November 1983 reaffirmed the U.S. security commitment to South Korea. What is perhaps more significant is the gradual and steady growth of trade and exchange of visitors between South Korea and China. In early 1985 one of the most prominent Korean businessmen made a secret visit to China. The two countries had unexpected political contacts when Chinese hijackers flew into South Korea in 1983 and when South Korea returned a Chinese patrol boat commandeered by mutineers in 1985. When the Japanese and Chinese leaders met during Hu Yaobang's trip to Tokyo in November 1983 and Nakasone's trip to Beijing in March 1984, they exchanged views on the Korean peninsula, agreeing on the need for a peaceful solution.

North Korea has traditionally been closer to China than to the USSR, and signs of increased North Korean-Soviet strains have recently been reported. President Kim Il Sung's May 1984 visit to Moscow, the first in 17 years, apparently was not fruitful for him, because the Soviets, it seems, neither provided a new military agreement nor endorsed Kim's son, Kim Jong Il, as his successor. As early as July 1983, China had apparently already endorsed the succession when Kim Jong Il made a secret trip to Beijing. And in early May 1984 Hu Yaobang succeeded in convincing Kim Il Sung, during his timely visit to Pyongyang just prior to Kim's departure for Moscow, that North Korea should shift its policy emphasis toward detente with South Korea and wider economic contacts with the West. Soon after Kim returned from the Soviet Union, he moved to follow Beijing's open-door foreign policy by introducing a foreign investment law, dispatching relief goods for South Korea's flood victims, and indicating, through his meetings with the visiting Japanese Socialist Party Chairman, that the North has no intention of forcing Communism on the South. The Soviet Union, apprehensive about closer links between North Korea and China, dispatched Vice Foreign Minister Mikhail Kapitsa to Pyongyang in late 1984, but his unusually long 14 day stay yielded little success for the Soviet Union. A border treaty was reached incorporating major Soviet concessions (which can be utilized by China and Japan in their claims to disputed territories), but there is no reason to suspect that North Korea agreed to Soviet use of its military facilities, ports, and airbases, especially at the very time when China was suggesting that it would agree to let U.S. warships visit Chinese ports.[3] During Kapitsa's stay in North Korea, a junior Soviet Embassy staff member defected through Panmunjom, but this incident did not block the new North-South dialogue. Before the end of Kapitsa's stay, President Kim left for Beijing, where he and the Chinese expressed their shared view that continuation of the dialogue across the 38th parallel was favorable, a view also supported by Japan and the United States.

As North Korea began its open-door policy in the fall of 1984, Japan decided to allow informal political contacts with North Korean officials. France made a successful bid for a contract to build a 50-story office/hotel building, the first joint venture since the foreign investment law in North Korea was issued. The French decided to allow an upgrading of North Korean representation in Paris from a commercial to general delegation. In January 1985 Tokyo officially lifted economic sanctions against North Korea that had been imposed after the Rangoon bombing; North Korea is trying to lure more Japanese capital to its shores through China. These moves greatly annoy Seoul. But they are likely to be successful in solidifying the North's still fragile posture of moderateness, which South Korea needs in order to ensure the success of the 1986 Asian Games and the 1988 Seoul Olympics. Despite deep suspicion of North Korea's intentions, Seoul has to keep the dialogue or at least the climate for it alive.

For Seoul, relations with the United States still remain essential, not only for its economic prosperity but for national security as well. At the same time, North Korea, although it argues in public that "U.S. imperialism" must leave the Peninsula, may also need the United States to restrain South Korea from taking military action against it. Moscow

---

[3]As of mid-1985 China is refusing to give permission for the visit of a U.S. naval ship until it is assured by Washington that the ship only carries conventional arms. During the late spring and the summer of 1985, Moscow provided MiG 23 fighters to Pyongyang and dispatched three naval ships to a North Korean port for a good will call. This indicates Soviet efforts to counter China's growing influence over North Korea, its approach to South Korea, and what Moscow often condemns as a U.S.-Japan-South Korea link of security activities. Historically, North Korea has often swung between Moscow and Beijing. It is important to note Moscow's active attempt to "encircle" China by strengthening military ties with North Korea as well as Vietnam, while advocating nonaligned relations with China.

and East European capitals, which, unlike Beijing, have so far refrained from committing themselves to the 1988 Seoul Olympics, nonetheless would like to avoid boycotting two Olympics in a row. They must thus exercise some restricting influence over Pyongyang so that they can come to Seoul in the same way as they attended the 1972 Munich Games, another Olympics held in a divided nation. Finally, by 1988, it is estimated, South Korea's military strength may surpass North Korea's, for the former has a growing defense industry backed by a high-growth economy. If all these factors should work in Seoul's favor, this would contribute to the stability of North-South relations in Korea. But Seoul must always keep in mind that without Moscow's encouragement Pyongyang could disrupt the process.

F. INDOCHINA

Unlike North Korea, Vietnam is currently an opportunist collaborator with Soviet expansionism in East Asia. With Soviet help, the military balance in Indochina is much more in favor of Hanoi than of Democratic Kampuchean and other anti-Hanoi forces in the Peninsula. Yet a host of economic and political problems plague Vietnam and Sino-Vietnamese rivalry is likely to aggravate Vietnam's domestic problems.

In November 1984 Vietnamese forces launched the sixth and largest dry-season offensive against the anti-Vietnamese coalition forces in Western Kampuchea since 1979. By early January 1985, with Soviet-supplied armored tanks and heavy artillery, the Vietnamese forces had taken Ampil, headquarters of Son Sann's Kampuchean People's National Liberation Front (KPNLF), one component of the tripartite coalition government of Democratic Kampuchea. The other two components are led by Prince Sihanouk and Khieu Samphan, the latter representing Pol Pot's Khmer Rouge. This has caused concern in China, which assembled forces, including for the first time its airforce, along the border with Vietnam. China threatened another "punitive war" against Hanoi in an attempt to check Vietnam's aggressive moves in Western Kampuchea. China also sent Foreign Minister Wu Xueqian to Bangkok to support Thai efforts to keep the anti-Vietnam Kampuchean resistance viable. The United States expressed concern about the situation along Thailand's eastern border and quickly reinforced arms supplies for the Thai military. Singapore's Prime Minister Lee Kuan Yew invited high ranking leaders of ASEAN countries along with former U.S. Secretary of State Henry Kissinger to his country to discuss the new Kampuchean situation and possibly to draw the United States more closely to the region. ASEAN foreign ministers met in an gency session in February 1985 and requested U.S. military aid for the non-Communist forces in Kampuchea.

From a military point of view, the anti-Vietnamese groups in Kampuchea, who number approximately 60,000 fighters, are poorly armed, despite Chinese help. Singapore is known to have shipped some 500 rifles in 1983 and some 3,000 AK47 rifles in 1984. But in terms of diplomatic relations, Democratic Kampuchea, led by President Sihanouk, Prime Minister Son Sann, and Vice Premier Khieu Samphan, is in a much better position than is the Vietnam-backed People's Republic of Kampuchea, which Heng Samrin heads. The former is recognized by some 72 countries, whereas the latter is recognized by only 33. ASEAN's position for keeping Democratic Kampuchea in the United Nations has enjoyed extensive international support, receiving 90 favorable votes in 1982. (This issue was not voted on in 1983 and 1984.) This gap between the military and diplomatic balance has been due in large part to the U.S. refusal to become involved militarily in the Peninsula. Only in April 1985 did the U.S. Congress vote to appropriate $5 million to promote the cause of Democratic Kampuchea. This is likely to include military hardware.

There have been several proposals for a political solution to the Kampuchean problem, including (1) a gradual replacement of Vietnamese troops by an international peace-keeping force and a U.N.-administered free election, (2) a coalition government under Sihanouk, Son Sann, and Heng Samrin, with or without Pol Pot, and (3) a coalition government under Heng Samrin and Sihanouk. But none of these plans is feasible as long as Vietnam and ASEAN, particularly Thailand, retain their respective positions: Vietnam wants a pro-Hanoi regime in Phnom Penh, whereas Thailand wants either an anti-Hanoi or a neutralist regime. Every year Vietnam gives a showy farewell ceremony for its "volunteer troops" withdrawing from Kampuchea in order to demonstrate that an "irreversible" situation is emerging under the "firmly-founded" Heng Samrin government and this is making the gradual withdrawal of Vietnamese troops possible. But the Vietnamese military presence still numbers 160,000 to 190,000 troops, and there is no sign that an actual significant withdrawal has been undertaken. Vietnam is definitely eager to keep Kampuchea under control for the sake of its national security and because of an historical sense of superiority over the Kampucheans as well as Laotians. Vietnam's attempts to assimilate Kampuchea are underway through migration, intermarriage, education, and so forth.

Vietnam's apparent intention to annex Kampuchea de facto will not go unresisted. Historically, Kampucheans are known to be tough nationalists, and they will continue to resist Vietnamese control. For its part, Hanoi will have to justify its control by using the Pol Pot massacre for propaganda purposes. For this reason, it will be in Hanoi's interest to keep some Pol Pot remnants alive rather than annihilating them. But as long as Pol Pot elements are alive, they will be helped by China to fight against the Vietnamese. Son Sann's and Sihanouk's non-Communist groups, being small and feeble, rely on the Pol Pot guerrillas for their own survival. Consequently, the present unstable situation is likely to continue. In the meantime, Hanoi will have to depend more heavily on Moscow for military supplies. Moscow uses this situation to expand its military stronghold in Vietnam and to link Vietnamese workers and food products to the development of the Soviet Far East.

Vietnam appears to have less contested control in Laos than over Kampuchea. It has stationed in Laos 40,000 to 60,000 troops, presumably under the bilateral 25-year Treaty of Friendship and Cooperation, concluded in July 1977. The Soviet presence comprised of military and other technical advisors is also impressive. To counterbalance Vietnam's and the Soviet Union's role, some democratic powers like Japan, France, Australia, and Sweden have tried to increase their influence through economic aid. Since 1983 the United States similarly has tried to improve relations with Vientiane. On the other hand, China provides some support for anti-government rebels. Thailand plays a unique role; the Laos are ethnically related to the Thais, and Laos' external economic relations still primarily depend on access to Bangkok. Thus, while a "special alliance" relationship among Vietnam, Laos, and Heng Samrin's Kampuchea is emerging and disguising Hanoi's patronage, major external powers are involved in Laos, and could possibly threaten Vietnamese domination.

Vietnam itself will continue to be an area of serious instability. One Western source claims that there is a growing tension within the government between those like Foreign Minister Nguyen Co Thach who favor peacefully negotiated settlements over Kampuchea and those like Party Secretary Le Duan and the military who want to continue to fight, but little is known about relationships within the Vietnamese elite. Hanoi's next generation of leaders is likely to be just as hard-core Russian-trained as its current aged Politburo members are. The traditional conflicts between Hanoi and Ho Chi Minh City remain unresolved, with the latter becoming once again the center of external trade, occasionally challenging the Hanoi leadership. Anti-Communist subversives have not been contained, as the public court trial in December 1984 of some 20 people revealed. Bureaucratic inefficiency and graft proliferate under poor economic management and infeasible regulations. Even those Vietnamese who were often selected by favoritism and sent to the Soviet Union and other COMECON countries for job training utilized their opportunities to smuggle in high quality foreign goods.

G. THE SOUTH CHINA SEA

The continued battle in Kampuchea, military intimidation from China, and domestic economic mismanagement, compounded by the cancellation of aid and investment by the major industrialized democracies, compel Vietnam to depend more upon the Soviet Union. This tendency is likely to deepen the Sino-Vietnamese rift. One factor has been disputed claims to the Paracels and Spratly Islands in the South China Sea, some of the latter of which are also claimed by Malaysia and the Philippines. While it seems unlikely that territorial disputes in these islands would be a cause of war or a source of major tensions in themselves, they can add to the list of grievances among governments and become an additional source of conflict where relations have already been poisoned. In the case of the South China Sea islands, they are extremely small and virtually uninhabitable, but their possession can affect important resource claims on the seabed. Because all governments are reluctant to relinquish claimed territory, it is likely these competing claims will persist for some time. A brief outline of the situation, therefore, is in order.

Traditionally, the two major island groups, the Paracels and Spratlys, were considered by most nations including Vietnam to be under Chinese jurisdiction. After 1949 both Beijing and Taipei claimed them. The situation became tense when during the late 1960s the area was thought to have oil reserves and the United Nations Conference on the Law of the Sea started to discuss law of the sea issues including the continental shelf rights and the exclusive economic zones. In 1973 South Vietnam issued exploration permits in the Spratlys, and set up a garrison in the Paracels. In January 1974 Chinese forces drove the South Vietnamese troops out of the Paracels, but within a month after the fall of Saigon North Vietnam occupied some of the Spratlys and also contested the claims on the Paracels by China and Taiwan.

In the ensuing years, as Beijing-Hanoi relations deteriorated, the territorial arguments became uncompromising. The situation today is actually even more complicated by the occupation of some islets in the Spratlys by the Philippines and Taiwan, disagreements on the delimitation line between China and Vietnam in the Gulf of Tonkin, and between Vietnam and Kampuchea on the Gulf of Siam. Indonesia and

Vietnam have an unsettled dispute over their shelf claims near the Natuna Islands, while Malaysia also continues to claim a few islets in the South China Sea. In the meantime, since the Sino-Vietnamese war of 1979, the Soviet air and naval forces, based in Danang and Cam Rahn Bay, have been periodically patrolling the South China Sea. In April 1984 the Soviet naval forces practiced amphibious landings near Haiphong, presumably to demonstrate to the Chinese the Soviet-Vietnamese capability to take over the Paracels. Reportedly this exercise prompted China to send warships into the area. China's acceptance of a U.S. warship call to Shanghai may be calculated to send a message to Moscow that U.S.-Chinese naval cooperation should not be discounted. The Chinese interest in building more than a coastal navy seems to be growing, as does the Vietnamese. The maritime tension between China and Vietnam can be aggravated in the future, affecting the security of the shipping route there.

V. Other Regional Instability Issues

A. SOURCES OF POLITICAL INSTABILITY

East Asian regional security is affected not solely by external factors, as has been discussed in the previous chapter, but also by internal factors in the region. Internal factors are often so intertwined with external factors that it is difficult to make a clear distinction. Yet, if the political and economic viability of any nation provides an essential basis for national security, inattention to internal sources of political instability would ignore a vital dimension of regional security.

Political instability and its potential are naturally both relative and somewhat subjective. Compared with other regions such as the Middle East and Central America, East Asia today has relatively few countries with actual instability. Examples of such countries are Kampuchea and the Philippines. Most other countries in East Asia may be discussed in terms of potential political instability.

Some factors which used to be a source of political instability have become less important. Communist subversion, for instance, is no longer so prevalent; it is even hard to imagine that most non-Communist countries in Southeast Asia, particularly Indonesia and Malaysia, once suffered severely from it. Today in Southeast Asia only the Philippines faces a serious challenge from indigenous Communists. Burma has a much less serious Communist threat. Apart from those countries, the rest of the Southeast Asian region has successfully contained local Communists who are keeping a low profile in part because of the demise of their popular support and in larger part because of China's tactical restraint. The enhanced standard of living based on a market economy has much to do with the loss of attraction of the Marxist economic model. If Southeast Asian economies should deteriorate in the future, as a result of protectionism in the U.S. economy, this would give the Communists an opportunity to advance their cause. Similarly, if China finds it useful to instigate local Communist rebellions, the latter may improve their positions, although Chinese ability to directly assist them is limited.

Inter-ethnic tension, another important source of potential instability, could still be a potentially large problem in Malaysia and Indonesia, where citizens of Chinese descent are wealthier than the rest of the population and often become targets of economic and political dissatisfaction. In Malaysia, where the Chinese account for 35 percent of the population, communal tensions have at times been very serious, but limitations imposed on public debate of sensitive issues has helped the Kuala Lumpur government to avoid a repetition of the bloody Malay-Chinese clashes of 1969. Burma has perennial ethnic conflict, primarily tensions between the Burmans, who constitute 70 percent of the population, and the rest of the population. But since 1962 the country has been held together under two retired generals, Ne Win and San Yu, both Burmans, while separatist movements in frontier regions have failed to make significant progress.

Armed Moslem dissidents have been active in the Philippines. In Malaysia and Indonesia, Islam is an important political force. Conservative Islamic fundamentalists, based in Kelantan on the northern Malay peninsula, have worked primarily through the Islamic Party, originally formed in 1950, but have suffered from periodic intra-party blood-letting. Yet the current radicals, some of whom were educated in Iran, are attempting to establish an Islamic state in Malaysia. That cause was shared by Indonesia's radical Moslems, typically represented by the Darul Islam members, who were active and imprisoned in the 1950s. Their successors began terrorist activities again in the late 1970s, including the hijacking of a plane in 1981. In 1984 Jakarta suffered a series of fires and bomb blasts that were attributed to radical Shiah Moslems dissatisfied with President Suharto's effort to secularize the Moslem party (PPP). The Khomeini revolution seems to have stimulated frustrated Moslems, who may grow stronger in the future if they feel that fundamental Islamic values are getting lost in a country where Islam is a dominant religion.

More immediate sources of political instability relate to uncertain political succession and economic mismanagement, both of which pose a more important challenge to the Northeast and Southeast Asian region.

1. Unpredictable Political Succession

Of the 15 nations in East Asia, in at least six countries, an uncertain political succession is a near-term prospect. They are China, North Korea, Taiwan, Indonesia, the Philippines, and Vietnam. The virtually permanent rule by the present leaders of these countries has created the facade of political stability. Kim Il Sung of North Korea is the longest power-holder at 40 years, being followed by Pham Van Dong of Vietnam and Ferdinand Marcos of the Philippines (see Table 8). Yet because the permanent rule by strong leaders has been made possible by driving out political opponents, usually by force, these leaders are often reluctant to set rules concerning the transition of power to their successors. Thus permanent rule itself becomes an element of political instability, as the procedure for political succession is uncertain. Among the current leaders of East Asia, only the leaders of Japan, Singapore, and Malaysia acquired and retained office through free elections. All the rest have done so by martial law, coup d'etat, revolution, heredity, or some untransparent procedure, although many of them subsequently have used general elections to shore up their political legitimacy. Marcos was initially elected through competitive procedures but subsequently stayed in power by undemocratic means.

TABLE 8

The Most Prominent Policy Makers of East Asia*

COUNTRY	NAME	FIRST DATE IN POWER	AGE (BIRTH YEAR)
China	Deng Xiaoping	1973	81 (1904)
	Hu Yaobang	1981	70 (1910)
	Zhao Ziyang	1980	66 (1919)
Japan	Nakasone Yasuhiro	1982	67 (1918)
North Korea	Kim Il Sung	1948	73 (1912)
South Korea	Chun Doo Hwan	1979	54 (1931)
Taiwan	Chiang Ching-kuo	1976	75 (1910)
Brunei	Hassanal Bolkiah	1968	38 (1947)
Burma	Ne Win	1958	74 (1911)
	San Yu	1981	67 (1918)
Indonesia	Suharto	1966	64 (1921)
Kampuchea(1)			
Laos	Kayson Phoumviharn	1975	65 (1920)
Malaysia	Mahathir	1981	60 (1925)
Philippines	Ferdinand E. Marcos	1966	68 (1917)
Singapore	Lee Kuan Yew	1959	62 (1923)
Thailand	Prem Tinsulanonda	1980	65 (1920)
Vietnam	Pham Van Dong	1954	79 (1906)
	Le Duan	1960	77 (1907)

*Those selected are customarily regarded as the primary national policy formulator in their respective countries, regardless of official status.

Note: (1) Due to the fluidity of the situation in Kampuchea, it is not sensible to list Heng Samrin, Sihanouk, Son Sann or Pol Pot along with other "national" leaders.

Most countries in East Asia have constitutions which stipulate the rules for selecting their leaders. But only Japan and Malaysia have constitutions specifying democratic rules for choosing political leaders and have actually practiced them. Countries like Singapore and South Korea have constitutional rules for competitive democratic procedures for political succession, but have never tested them against actual succession cases. This alone makes political succession highly unpredictable. The military, which is outside the constitutional process, actually plays a dominant political role in countries such as Burma, Thailand, and Indonesia, not to mention the Communist countries. President Chun Doo Hwan's term as President of South Korea will expire in late February 1988, just a few months before the Seoul Olympics begin. The argument that it would be undesirable to have a period of any political tension before the international games may justify the prolongation of his presidency, even at the cost of violating the constitutional provisions. President Suharto of Indonesia will complete his fourth five-year term in 1988, but his past three nominations, namely, the ones in 1969, 1973, and 1983, were made in the absence of any formal contender for the People's Consultative Congress (MPR) to consider. President Chiang Ching-kuo of Taiwan and President Marcos of the Philippines have followed more or less the same pattern. No East Asian Communist governments (China, North Korea, Laos and Vietnam) have revealed the procedures they will follow to determine who will succeed their current top leaders. North Korea's Kim Il Sung's unusual efforts to choose his own son as a hereditary successor may not succeed. The death of Deng Xiaoping may weaken the political base of Hu Yaobang and Zhao Ziyang.

The problem of succession is complicated by the fact that many of the East Asian leaders are over 65 (see Table 8). Those who are in their late 70s include Deng Xiaoping, Pham Van Dong, Le Duan, and Chiang Ching-kuo. Thus transitions in political leadership should occur in several countries within the coming decade. Whether the successors will be as capable of governing their countries remains to be seen.

2. Economic Mismanagement

Economic mismanagement can exacerbate problems such as low economic growth, inflation, unemployment, unequal distribution of national income, trade deficits, and, more currently, foreign debts. These may be sources of social and political tensions. Moreover, the economic growth process itself may aggravate political and social problems.

At present the economies of non-Communist East Asia are healthy except for the Philippine and perhaps Thai economies (see Table 9). Despite large trade deficits and foreign debts, the South Korean economy remains strong because of active exports. The global glut of oil has led to stagnation in the Indonesian economy for the last few years; however, it is still in fair condition, although some radical Moslems feel frustrated because Indonesia's economy depends too much upon the economies of the advanced industrial nations. One important factor that keeps the region economically successful is its relatively good security environment, which keeps national defense a relatively low priority and allows for high priority to be given to economic development.

What is uncertain is the future of the Chinese economy. As was referred to in the previous chapter, it is growing fast under the pragmatic directorship of Deng Xiaoping and Hu Yaobang. But can it develop in a balanced way? In early 1985 the leaders, already acknowledging

TABLE 9

External Public Debt Outstanding* of East Asian Countries
(in million U.S. dollars)

	1980	1981	1982	1983
Burma	5,486.2	6,174.8	6,996.0	n.a.
Hong Kong	1,099.7	351.8	289.7	233.0
Indonesia	24,353.8	27,091.5	30,740.5	34,528.1
ROK	22,339.9	24,915.6	26,213.7	n.a.[1]
Malaysia	5,532.7	6,943.9	9,353.0	12,652.2
Philippines	10,761.8	12,496.6	13,907.4	14,834.5[2]
Singapore	1,592.9	1,586.7	1,834.5	1,588.6
Taiwan	5,704.1	6,146.9	7,187.9	7,094.1
Thailand	7,127.4	8,264.5	9,788.3	10,485.2

*Including undisbursed

Notes: (1) Economic Planning Board announced that the ROK's external debt outstanding as of the end of 1983 reached $40.1 billion.
(2) Quarterly Report (October 1983) of the Central Bank of the Philippines quoted $25.6 billion as accumulated external debt of the country, public and private, as of the end of 1983.

Source: Based on figures presented in Asian Development Bank's *Key Indicators of Developing Member Countries of ADB* (October 1984).

that the economy's 1984 growth rate of 14 percent was too fast, expressed the need to slow down the economy. The reported gap in personal income between the poor rural and the rich urban sectors may cause political tensions. Should China fail to produce internationally competitive goods, it would not be able to export them. That, in turn, would make it difficult for China to repay the interest on the foreign credits it has obtained. A politically unstable China caused by economic mismanagement will have serious consequences for the regional security environment. To a much lesser extent but still significantly, the economic mismanagement of North Korea and Vietnam, which is symbolized by their low economic growth and accumulated foreign debt, may also drive them to more militant external behavior.

B. THE CASE OF THE PHILIPPINES

At present the Philippines possesses all the elements of political instability discussed previously: political succession, economic mismanagement, Communist subversion, Islamic separatism, and military corruption. The assassination of former Senator Benigno Aquino in August 1983 heightened political tensions and accelerated the pace of political instability. This situation has become of concern to all the East Asian non-Communist countries, and to the United States which has major naval and air force base facilities in the country.

Ailing Ferdinand Marcos, who is now 68 years old and who took over power in 1966 by popular election, placed the country under martial law between 1972 and 1981. In December 1983, he established the constitutional provisions for selecting a successor but has made no obvious attempt to groom anyone. The question is not only who will be chosen through this constitutional procedure, but whether the constitutional procedure will actually be applied. Mrs. Imelda Marcos, who in 1983 explicitly indicated her intention not to succeed her husband, is nonetheless seen as a major contender. General Fabian Ver, who has lost at least temporarily his position as Chief of Staff of the 90,000-man Philippine armed forces because of his alleged complicity in the Aquino assassination, has been known as a trusted confidant of Marcos and has been close to Mrs. Marcos also. This connection will make Mrs. Marcos' candidacy for president even more unpopular among the students, young businessmen, and Catholic Church leaders. Prime Minister Cesar Virata is a respected technocrat, but is not considered to have much taste for politics. General Fidel Ramos, who has taken over Ver's post temporarily, is reportedly trying to "clean up" the military establishment from corruption, brutality, and favoritism, but is not regarded as a presidential aspirant. The democratic opposition contains a number of potential aspirants—Salvador Laurel, Aquilino Pimentel, Agapito Aquino, and Lorenzo Tanada, to name just some of the more prominent. This opposition shows little ability to unite around anything but their common desire to see Marcos leave the scene. Under these circumstances, Marcos' prolonged life helps forestall a struggle for power, postponing the constitutional and political crisis.

Despite Virata's tireless efforts, the Philippine economy has worsened over the last several years. The average annual growth rate for 1978-81 in real terms was 5.4 percent but that for 1984 was estimated to be -3 percent to -6 percent. The annual rate of inflation is 50 percent. Foreign exchange reserves went down from $2,540 million in 1982 to $400 million in 1983. Manila's total foreign debt outstanding, public and private, is now about $26 billion, some 70 percent of its GNP. When it could not pay the interest for a $14.8 billion debt outstanding in October 1983, it became the first East Asian country in recent years to ask that payments be rescheduled. Since then, payments have been rescheduled four times, the last time in December 1984. The IMF instituted strict conditions for economic austerity programs, but the regime's weakness inhibits its ability to implement these effectively. The economy will not grow until more goods are produced at home to control the inflation.

The widespread military abuses committed by the corrupt, undisciplined soldiers of the Philippine Army and the growing disparity of national income between rich and poor are certainly helping the cause of the illegal Communist Party (CCP) and its armed wing, the New People's Army (NPA). Unlike in other ASEAN countries, the Communists are active and growing in the Philippines. According to government estimates, the NPA has expanded from some 3,000 men in 1983 to nearly 8,000 at present. The NPA itself claims approximately 20,000 guerrillas, of whom 10,000 are armed, and a mass base of some 1 million, who are active in two-thirds of the country's provinces. The Communists are also moving into urban areas. Some Catholic priests, influenced by Liberation Theology, are working with the NPA. One source claims that Cubans are also seen working in the villages. Although they are far from being strong enough to topple the government, the NPA's daring terrorist actions alarm those concerned with the nation's internal security.

The Islamic Moro ethnic groups in Mindanao, a large southern island with rich natural resources, do not challenge the position of the authorities in Manila, but have been a hotbed of unrest in the South.

East Asian Security

The Moro National Liberation Front (MNLF), which was active in the 1970s, has lost much of its momentum because many of its leaders have either surrendered, been coopted or killed, and outside arms supplies, financed by Libya and transported through Malaysia, have been much reduced. The leadership, however, remains in contact with Libya and collaboration with the NPA is reported from time to time.

There is no evidence of Soviet aid to the MNLF and NPA, but Moscow has been courting the government in Manila because it wants to weaken Manila-Washington ties. No break between Washington and Manila is foreseeable now, as the latter depends upon the former in virtually all respects. The United States is aware of this and hopes to maneuver economic and political developments in the Philippines in ways that meet its national interests, which are to retain its largest overseas bases and to encourage the development of democratic institutions. The United States is anxious to avoid seeing the Philippines following Nicaragua or Iran. While this does not seem likely, there is a potential for the emergence of leadership hostile to Washington and to the continued presence of U.S. bases. Whether or not such leadership developed alternative ties with the Soviet Union, the loss of the base facilities in themselves would be a major blow to U.S. and trilateral strategic interests in the region.

VI. PROSPECTS FOR ARMS CONTROL IN EAST ASIA

"Arms control" is a somewhat novel concept in East Asia. "Regional balance" and "regional security" have been more common notions. Only in recent years has "arms control" begun to be recognized as an issue; the Soviet deployment in Asia and the Pacific of SS-20 missiles, Backfire bombers, and nuclear-armed warships have contributed to this new interest.

A. NUCLEAR ARMS CONTROL

The concern about heightened nuclear tension in Northeast Asia can hardly lead to negotiations, as such concern did in Europe. First of all, deployments of nuclear forces in East Asia are far more asymmetrical. The Soviet land-based ICBMs in the Soviet Far East cannot be traded for the untrackable U.S. submarine-based ballistic missiles. Second, since both the United States and the Soviet Union have a policy of not disclosing whether ships, planes, and cruise missiles such as Tomahawks carry nuclear arms, they cannot start negotiations on how to control them. If the United States should disclose the whereabouts of its nuclear arms, it might seriously strain relations with some allies, particularly Japan. Third, both the United States and the Soviet Union will have difficulty deciding how to treat China's nuclear arms. Neither side would feel comfortable claiming them for their own side.

The difficulty of verification and the mutual desire for non-disclosure of the whereabouts of nuclear weapons undermine the incentive for nuclear arms control in East Asia. What has proven feasible so far in this field, though still in a limited way, are unilateral and multilateral restraints on nuclear deployment, nuclear possession, and nuclear transfer. Since 1967, Japan has adopted a unilateral policy of what is known as the three non-nuclear principles: a policy against possessing nuclear arms, manufacturing nuclear arms, and allowing nuclear arms to be introduced into Japan. The third principle contradicts Japan's other policy of accepting American nuclear protection. The

TABLE 10

Major Multilateral Arms Control Agreements and East Asian Countries
(dates of ratification)
(as of December 31, 1983)

	GENEVA PROTOCOL (1925)	ANTARCTIC TREATY (1959)	PARTIAL TEST BAN TREATY (1963)	OUTER SPACE TREATY (1967)	TREATY OF TLATELOLCO (1967)
Burma			1963	1970	
China	1929	1983		1983	P II 1974
Indonesia	1971		1964	S	
Japan	1970	1960	1964	1967	
Kampuchea	1983				
ROK			1964	1967	
Laos			1965	1972	
Malaysia	1970		1964	S	
Philippines	1973		1965	S	
Singapore			1968	1976	
Taiwan	1929		1964	1970	
Thailand	1931		1963	1968	
Vietnam	1980			1980	

*China signed safeguard agreement with IAEA in 1984.

Notes: S: Signature without further action.
   SA: Safeguards agreement in force with the International Atomic Energy
   Agency under the Non-Proliferation Treaty or the Treaty of Tlatelolco,
   which provides IAEA with authority to verify signees' nuclear energy
   program in order to prevent diversion of nuclear energy from peaceful uses
   to nuclear weapons or other nuclear explosive devices.
   P II: Additional protocol II to the Treaty of Tlatelolco.

Source: *SIPRI Yearbook 1984.*

TABLE 10 (Continued)

Major Multilateral Arms Control Agreements and East Asian Countries
(dates of ratification)
(as of December 31, 1983)

	NPT (1968)	SEA-BED TREATY (1971)	BIOLOGICAL WEAPON CONVENTION (1972)	ENVIRONMENTAL MODIFICATION TECHNIQUES CONVENTION (1977)	INHUMANE WEAPONS CONVENTION (1981)
Burma		S	S		
China	*				1982
Indonesia	1979 SA		S		
Japan	1976 SA	1971	1982	1982	1982
Kampuchea	1972	S	1983		
ROK	1975 SA	S	S		
Laos	1970	1971	1973	1978	1983
Malaysia	1970 SA	1972	S		
Philippines	1972 SA		1973		S
Singapore	1976 SA	1976	1975		
Taiwan	1970	1972	1973		
Thailand	1972 SA		1975		
Vietnam	1982	1980	1980	1980	S

*China signed safeguard agreement with IAEA in 1984.

Notes: S: Signature without further action.
SA: Safeguards agreement in force with the International Atomic Energy Agency under the Non-Proliferation Treaty or the Treaty of Tlatelolco, which provides IAEA with authority to verify signees' nuclear energy program in order to prevent diversion of nuclear energy from peaceful uses to nuclear weapons or other nuclear explosive devices.
P II: Additional protocol II to the Treaty of Tlatelolco.

Source: *SIPRI Yearbook 1984.*

apparent contradiction continues to be a source of political tension in Japan. In spite of the apparent contradiction, the two policies coexist. Japan's Basic Law on Atomic Power, enacted in 1955, also stipulates that it shall use nuclear energy "solely for peaceful purposes."

Both the Korean and Vietnam Wars were limited to conventional weapons, reflecting the United States unilateral restraint. Washington also has national legislation that prohibits nuclear proliferation to foreign countries. These unilateral restraints have contributed to creating a climate favorable to mutual restraint in Asia. Potential nuclear powers such as South Korea and Taiwan might have gone nuclear if Japan had. It is significant that Japan, even though it has the technological capability to produce nuclear arms, has declined to join the nuclear club.

There are several multilateral agreements for nuclear restraint in which East Asian countries have participated (see Table 10). They include the Partial Test Ban Treaty of 1963, the Outer Space Treaty of 1967, the Nuclear Non-Proliferation Treaty (NPT) of 1970, and the International Atomic Energy Agency (IAEA) Charter of 1957. Most of the non-Communist countries of East Asia, including Japan, are parties to all of these agreements. China pointedly refused to join any of them until late 1984. That year China agreed that on-site inspection by the IAEA would be conducted to ensure that its imported nuclear energy was being used for peaceful aims only. In early 1984 Vietnam, with Soviet and IAEA assistance, reactivated the nuclear reactor the United States left behind in 1975. China has declared that it will not proliferate nuclear technology. It has yet to become a party to the NPT, and it is feared that nuclear materials sold to China might be transferred to Pakistan for the development of nuclear arms. The need to persuade China to join the NPT is urgent.

Another multilateral agreement for nuclear non-proliferation relates to the idea of a nuclear-free zone. In 1982, Indonesia proposed a nuclear-free zone for Southeast Asia at the U.N. Conference on Disarmament, and two years later, in September 1984, Malaysia reiterated that proposal after a decision was made in late August that year to establish a South Pacific nuclear-free zone. Both of these proposals are unfeasible. A Southeast Asia nuclear-free zone was raised within the context of the ASEAN declaration in 1971 for establishing "a zone of peace, freedom, and neutrality" (ZOPFAN) in Southeast Asia. The nuclear-free zone would be impossible without closing U.S. bases in the Philippines and banning Soviet use of bases in Vietnam, or without the Philippines taking action similar to New Zealand regarding the use of its ports by U.S. warships that may carry nuclear arms.

B. CONVENTIONAL ARMS CONTROL

As in the case of nuclear arms, there also exist no regional agreements on conventional arms control for East Asia. There has been no East Asian version of the European attempt, though not yet successful, for a mutual reduction of force and armament. The concept of mutual balanced force reduction (MBFR) is based on the balance between the two formal alliances, NATO and the Warsaw Treaty Organization, in which both sides recognize each other's military presence and in which they would feel more secure by reducing their arms. The MBFR is also based on the assumption that along the demarcation line both sides have or can have, after a reduction of forces, relatively symmetrical force deployments of more or less equal significance to their respective security. Very few places in East Asia resemble the situation in Central Europe.

There are several areas within the region where adversarial military concentrations exist: the Sino-Soviet border, the Sino-Vietnamese border, the Thai-Kampuchean border, and the North Korean-South Korean border. Arms control measures are hardly feasible for any one of them. The Sino-Soviet border is too long. Both sides have to find pertinent border areas for arms reduction. The border between Mongolia and China or that with northeastern China will need force reduction. But in either case the Soviets have an advantage because Moscow is farther from the border than Beijing. With superior arms the Soviets can still attack Beijing, but the Chinese cannot attack Moscow. Even after an agreement, the two countries would not have an equal sense of security. At the Sino-Vietnamese border, the situation is similar, except it is the Chinese who would have an advantage. Any arms reduction along the border is likely to present a greater security risk for Hanoi than for Beijing. The situation along the Thai-Kampuchean border is too complicated to warrant arms control. The natural setting, the jungles and forests, makes it difficult to control the movement of troops, particularly armed guerrillas. Active in the border area are several military groups, including the three anti-Vietnamese guerrilla groups, which the Thai forces are not in a position to control. Thai-Vietnamese talks on arms reduction or disengagement would be fruitless. Only the Korean peninsula comes close to the Central European situation. In fact, the 38th parallel border, being clearly set, makes it easier for mutual arms reduction talks to be held. But even the initiation of discussions, much more their successful conclusion, requires a prior political compromise between North and South. A distinctive difficulty is the fact that the two Koreas do not recognize each other.

The absence of conventional arms control agreements in East Asia should not be interpreted to mean that the region is a lawless jungle of formidable arms. The major powers have actually restrained their use of arms in the region. In the 1979 Sino-Vietnamese conflict, both sides chose not to employ air power. There are grounds to believe that both the Soviet Union and the United States are also cautious in choosing the kinds of arms they transfer to their partners in Korea. This suggests the traditional concept of arms control stressing formal agreements is not necessarily applicable to Asia. More useful is a tacit understanding among the parties involved on the wisdom of mutual restraint before and when tensions mount.

Some unilateral policies and a multilateral agreement are significant enough to be noted. Several suppliers of arms have unilateral policies of restricting any further transfer to a third country. The United States in particular stipulates that the arms it supplies only be used for certain purposes and prohibits those arms to be re-exported to a third country without its consent. Japan follows the most strict unilateral control policy. It adopted in 1967 three principles of arms export control based on the Export Trade Control Ordinance of 1949. The 1967 policy was further tightened in 1976. The result has been a prohibition of all arms sales to any country. One exception was allowed in 1983—that arms technology could be exported to the United States.

C. CONFIDENCE-BUILDING MEASURES: ASIAN TYPES

One way to reduce military tensions is through confidence-building measures (CBMs). In a European setting, as incorporated in the Helsinki Accord of 1975, such measures have included mutual notification of military maneuvers, exchange of observers for military maneuvers, and exchange of military hardware information. There have been a few similar proposals for the East Asian region, but none of them has been implemented so far. In 1981, the Soviet Union, for instance, made a CBM proposal to Japan, which refused to take interest in it because Tokyo considered the mutual notification of military maneuvers to be tactically designed to establish Japan's de facto recognition of a right for Soviet troops to be deployed in the disputed Northern Territories east of Hokkaido. Similarly, when Moscow made a CBM proposal to Beijing in 1984, the latter refused to consider it, for such a measure contradicted one of its three conditions for normalizing relations with Moscow-namely, that Soviet troop strength near the Chinese border be reduced. The Americans also proposed in the last few years that North Korea and China send observers to the annual U.S.-South Korea joint exercises, called Team Spirit. Pyongyang refused because it did not want to appear to be accepting the U.S. military presence in South Korea. The European model of confidence-building measures assumes that both parties recognize each other and accept each other's military presence. It loses its applicability in many areas in East Asia. One of the few European types of CBMs that have worked in the region is the "hot line" established between North and South Korea in 1971. It is a rather exceptional case, and perhaps it exists only because there are no diplomatic relations between them.

What is more acceptable in the region are political declarations of mutual or self-restraint. They have taken different forms. In 1954, when India's Prime Minister Nehru met China's Zhou Enlai, they adopted as the basis of interstate relations "five principles of peace," which China has since claimed as the basis of its foreign policy. The five principles refer to mutual respect for territorial integrity and sovereignty; non-aggression; non-interference in internal affairs; equality and mutual benefit; and peaceful coexistence. In 1960, China signed a non-aggression pact incorporating these principles with Burma which remains in effect. Japan has also adopted a policy of military restraint under its 1947 Constitution which denounces the right of belligerency. This has been further elaborated by its 1976 policy of keeping defense costs below one percent of GNP; and by frequent policy statements, most notably the one by Prime Minister Fukuda in 1977 in Manila, in which he declared that Japan would never become a military power. Japan's pledge to never again wage war with China made in 1984 in Nakasone's speech in Beijing, in addition to the 1978 Treaty of Peace and Friendship between the two countries, can also be seen in this context.

These diplomatic efforts that aim at creating a cordial climate are significant measures for building mutual confidence. There have been multilateral calls of a similar nature in Southeast Asia. As early as in 1955, the Asia-Africa Conference held in Bandung, Indonesia, adopted a declaration advocating the "ten principles of peace" based on Nehru's Five Principles of Peace. The ten principles endorsed a disavowal of ties with the big powers and advocated restraint on the use of force. This idea and the conference, signifying the beginning of the non-aligned movement, had an impact on the ASEAN declaration in 1971 for ZOPFAN, mentioned earlier. The ASEAN heads of state or government further signed an Accord of Peace and Amity in 1976 for the same purpose. In mid-1978, both China and the Soviet Union supported the notion of a Southeast Asian ZOPFAN, as did Vietnam. The Soviet-Vietnam alliance treaty, concluded only a few months later, changed this cordial climate. Confidence-building measures require a political accommodation. CBMs in Europe were a reflection of the atmosphere of detente in the early and mid-1970s.

The lack of resemblance in geographical features and in the force deployment pattern between Europe and East Asia thus calls for different approaches to arms control issues. Rather than trying to prohibit the kinds and levels of arms, the region may find it more productive to try to create a political climate which induces the concerned parties to reduce arms and yet feel secure. Or at least the parties may be better off trying to achieve tacit understanding about the need for mutual unilateral restraint of arms deployment rather than trying to reach a formal agreement on arms control.

VII. TOWARD TRILATERAL PARTNERSHIP IN EAST ASIA

The Soviets are building up forces in Asia. The massive economy of China has begun to move. Japan's economic and technological capabilities are affecting the world economy. Trade volume among the countries of East Asia and the Pacific is growing. Consequently the strategic importance of the Pacific and Indian Oceans has increased. The United States is a superpower that must keep a watchful eye on the global East-West relationship and the security of the different regions around the world, and it has now to pay closer attention to the East Asian region than before. Limited as Canada's power is, it is also shifting the balance of its foreign involvements from the Atlantic to the Pacific. West Europeans, on the other hand, are more concerned with other regions such as Eastern Europe, the Middle East, and Africa than with East Asia. Because of their regional orientation, they are bound to look upon security issues in Japan, China, or East Asia as a whole, as secondary in importance to the classic East-West relationship in Europe. They fear that the United States may be attaching too much importance to East Asia and the Pacific at the expense of Europe. These differences should be resolved within the broader common interests of the trilateral nations, or at least should be acknowledged as such.

The desirability of close Japan-United States discussions of Northeast and Southeast Asian issues is generally recognized and has been frequently discussed in governmental and private circles. The major danger is that Western European and Canadian roles and contributions in this region may be neglected, by the Europeans and Canadians themselves as well as by Americans and Japanese. This report has stressed that *the dynamic East Asian region involves the interests of all the trilateral partners.*

There needs to be *better understanding among the trilateral countries of their mutual and individual interests in East Asia and improved consultations to make their partnership more meaningful in the region.* It is, of course, neither desirable nor feasible to design a common strategy involving tight coordination and control of each other's East Asian policies. It is desirable that habits of regular trilateral consultations on major issues be developed, that there be better appreciation of common interests and that there be some coordination in the use of resources—economic and political—to more efficiently promote these interests. The trilateral countries share important values and interests globally; their efforts as global partners to promote democratic values, the respect of human rights, freedom from external coercion, and open trade and capital systems should be recognized as applying to East Asia as well as other areas. At important trilateral meetings, such as the Seven Nation Summits, East Asia should regularly receive multilateral attention and not be thought to be the interest of only one or two countries.

It should be recognized, of course, that *not all trilateral countries need to be involved in all major issues and certainly not in the same way. Each country's policy emphases in the region are affected by such factors as its historical relationships, its geographical characteristics, and peculiarities of its domestic situation including ethnic ties. Such discrepancies should be accepted if they are within a common trilateral frame of reference of broad interests and values. Those within and without such a frame should be distinguished.* In the pages that follow, policy approaches toward major issues of bearing to the trilateral partnership in general will be discussed.

A. STRATEGIC AND INTERMEDIATE-RANGE NUCLEAR FORCES

Among the trilateral countries, the United States should bear primary responsibility, after consultation with the other key trilateral partners, in maintaining the global strategic and INF balance and in negotiating nuclear arms control terms with the Soviet Union. Since the deployment of nuclear forces by both the United States and the Soviet Union in East Asia is coupled with the security of the European countries and Canada, Europeans and Canadians should also regard this regional balance as important to their security. Japan, being in the region, naturally has to take a great interest in the nuclear balance, particularly the Soviet SS-20 missiles, in East Asia. The important function of Europe, Canada, and Japan then is to show united support of the U.S. position vis-a-vis the Soviet Union, once consultation has taken place, lest the Soviet Union plays off its two fronts against each other. Moscow has a record of trying to divide the United States and its allies, thereby undermining Washington's negotiating positions.

B. CONVENTIONAL BALANCE

The United States should continue to play a vital role in maintaining the conventional arms balance with the Soviet Union by maintaining its bases in Japan, South Korea, the Philippines, and Australia, and by modernizing its forces to match those of the USSR. Canada and Western Europe are not expected to play a direct military role in East Asia, but Britain's participation in the Manila Pact and the Five-Power Defense Arrangement as well as its military presence in Hong Kong (until 1997) should be noted and continued. West European training of East Asian officers has been valuable and ought to be continued. Japan, for its part, should accelerate its arms modernization program and strengthen its self-defense capability, thus giving additional substance to Japan-U.S. security cooperation, which is the core for Asia-Pacific security. Canada's traditional international peace-keeping role should continue to be encouraged.

An appropriate level of Sino-American military cooperation will be beneficial for East Asian and trilateral security. But Washington should be cautious in promoting military cooperation with Beijing for this has already made the ASEAN nations and Japan apprehensive. Japan and some European nations feel uneasy because too close military cooperation between the United States and China could provoke the Soviet Union.

C. CHINA

China needs special attention from the trilateral governments. The trilateral nations agree on its strategic importance to global security and trade, but disagree as to how strong such a China should be. Perhaps even more essentially, they should first agree on whether or not they should treat China as a member of their extended partnership. China itself is ambivalent on this. While pessimistic, skeptical, and optimistic views coexist regarding China's future ability to govern itself, the trilateral countries and other countries as well should assist China's stable political and economic development.

At the same time the trilateral nations should find some way to avoid unnecessary mutual competition in providing for China certain critical technologies such as computers and nuclear energy development. Japan should avoid giving its European and North American partners the impression that "a Japanese-Chinese coprosperity sphere" may be on the rise.

D. KOREA

The Korean issue is likewise very much connected with the strategic environment of the region and with trilateral security. The past division of trilateral roles appears sound: namely, the military role is played primarily by Washington, and the political roles are played primarily by Washington and Tokyo, while other trilateral countries play an economic role. However, as North Korea appears to be seeking foreign investment, the trilateral nations, particularly the European nations, must not neglect the political and security implications of new economic relationships they may develop with the North. They should refrain from increasing political and economic contacts with Pyongyang to the extent that Seoul feels threatened. The United States should consult with other trilateral governments, Japan in particular, on any future significant changes in its military and political policies toward the Peninsula. Japan's role in retaining low-level non-political contacts with North Korea should be continued, for its possible moderating influence on the external behavior of the latter, which seeks Japanese goods and capital. The trilateral countries should encourage the North-South dialogue to become more meaningful and should work to create an international climate favorable for holding the Seoul Olympics in 1988, by ensuring Soviet participation, for instance.

E. INDOCHINA

Indochina seems to require even closer trilateral attention, for there are no common positions except on refugees. On the Kampuchean issue the postures of the trilateral countries are in near disarray. Trilateral governments have given support to the ASEAN position calling for a phased Vietnamese troop withdrawal and a neutralist government in Phnom Penh. But they have different policies on the recognition of Democratic Kampuchea and different political stances toward Hanoi.

The trilateral countries should handle their political and economic contacts with Vietnam with care, so as not to undermine ASEAN's, especially Thailand's, position vis-a-vis Hanoi. Because of historical ties, France may be able to play a useful political role here. Although Indochina is a strategically important region and is seen clearly as an area of East-West competition, the United States is reluctant to play a direct military and political role there. The Kampuchean problem and the growing Soviet presence in the peninsula and the South China Sea require a more active U.S. diplomatic role in defending the ASEAN's position on Kampuchea, supporting Kampuchean resistance, and restraining Vietnamese and Soviet military moves in Southeast Asia. Excessive American involvement in Vietnam, as in the 1960s, worked against Washington's interests and invited criticisms from U.S. allies, whereas too little involvement, as at present, simply gives freedom of action to the Vietnamese military in Indochina and the Soviet military in the region.

F. ISSUES OF POLITICAL INSTABILITY

Domestic instability carries a risk of external interference and even escalation into an East-West conflict. Where the Philippines is concerned, since the United States has had close "special" historical relations with it, the United States is expected to continue to play a major political role in keeping the Philippine issue out of East-West conflicts and in bringing about democratic institution-building. But there are limits to what Washington can and should do. Other trilateral nations should continue to coordinate their activities with the United States in helping to solve the negative consequences of economic mismanagement such as increased foreign debt, decreased foreign exchange revenue, a high rate of inflation, the widening gap between rich and poor, and the like.

Indonesia's problems of regime legitimacy and foreign debts are still more potential problems than actual ones. But this country could become a source of regional instability. If such a situation should develop, there is no single trilateral country that can play as direct a role there as America does in the Philippines. Probably Tokyo, Washington, and Canberra would have to assume a joint political and economic role.

Needless to say, external powers should avoid domestic interference, for example, in issues of political succession, interparty and intraparty disputes, and constitutional procedures. But the trilateral countries, especially those in North America and Western Europe, feel an urge to intervene to strengthen democratic processes and "correct" human rights violations. They should instead take a long-term and evolutionary view of democratic developments in the Third World and use a balanced approach. To emphasize a democratic process where there is low national consensus on it tends to lead to political instability and invite authoritarian control. Authoritarian control, on the other hand, tends to ensure political order, imperative for economic development, although it is apt to suppress human rights. A skillful balanced approach is required.

G. REGIONAL ARMS CONTROL

East Asia, being different from Europe in terms of geography and power alignments, calls for a different set of arms control measures. As a dominant military power in the region, the United States should play a decisive role in this field, too. Japan has hitherto neglected its role, but it should make efforts to study and propose those arms control measures workable in East Asia, particularly the kinds of confidence-building measures discussed in Chapter VI. If Japan, together with other trilateral countries, could also persuade China to accede to the Nuclear Non-Proliferation Treaty, it would certainly contribute to alleviating apprehensions about the future transfer of nuclear energy capabilities.

H. "THE PACIFIC BASIN COMMUNITY"

The trilateral countries should share the view that prosperous Pacific economic growth can be beneficial to all of them if properly managed. The United States, Japan, and Canada should make greater efforts to keep the emerging new community open in terms of membership. They should avoid building a formal institutional framework for the Pacific. Fifteen to twenty potential member nations of widely different characters would make only an ineffective institution. The membership question also inevitably involves complicated issues of Taiwan, North and South Korea, and so forth. The United States, Japan, and Canada should encourage their European partners to be more actively involved in the Pacific economy.

In the meantime, a major issue today is the upsurge of trade problems between Japan and its trilateral partners, especially the United States, and between Japan and many East Asian countries such as South Korea, the Philippines, and Thailand. Japan and the United States bear the primary responsibility for reducing their mutual trade imbalance, by readjusting dollar-yen exchange rates and industrial structures and by reducing trade barriers. The Pacific powers, particularly Japan, should make strenuous efforts in adjusting industrial structures to buy goods from the NICs and ASEAN nations. European roles continue to be important in promoting their exports.

I. MECHANISMS FOR TRILATERAL COORDINATION

No trilateral consultation or coordination is possible without appropriate machinery. Nor will communication necessarily flow smoothly unless channels of communication are established in advance, for critical events may require quick responses. Issues of East Asian security are too complex and multidimensional to be handled by any single mechanism. Given the fact that there exist already quite a few mechanisms for communication and that any consultation involves more time from already pressed high-ranking leaders, attempts should be made to make use of and improve the existing arrangements rather than to create new ones.

Some of the more useful mechanisms may be cited here. The annual Seven-Nation Summit could discuss the issues of strategic force balance as they relate to East Asia as well as China and the future of the Pacific basin. The ASEAN annual foreign ministers conference, to which are invited counterparts from the United States, Canada, Japan, and the EC (President of the Council of Ministers) as well as Australia and New Zealand, has discussed refugees, Kampuchea, the Soviet presence in Southeast Asia, and Pacific basin cooperation, although the last without European participation. This meeting does not always have a sufficiently strong European input. But there are ASEAN-EC ministerial meetings as well, which might be strengthened.

Many trilateral nations participate in economic aid and debt payment programs through the OECD, the World Bank and the International Monetary Fund (IMF), the Asian Development Bank, and the U.N. specialized agencies such as the Economic and Social Commission for Asia and the Pacific. Their interests are also expressed through bilateral contacts with the governments of East Asia and international consortia such as those for the Philippines and Indonesia. These economic aid organizations and mechanisms are presumably sufficient to meet the needs of the region. Perhaps some of them should even be dissolved to eliminate interorganizational redundancy, rivalry, and resultant inefficiency.

Where China is concerned, the Coordinating Committee for Export Control (COCOM), which is composed of Japan and all NATO nations except Iceland and Spain, could improve the process for giving permits for selling "strategic export items" to China. U.S. and Japanese specialists on China periodically meet to compare notes; this might be extended to include other countries as well. With regard to Korea, the ambassadors of trilateral governments in Seoul could informally consult occasionally on developments in the Peninsula so that they have better understanding of them.

For the foreseeable future, East Asia will be a vital region of the world, which no major nation can ignore. Both optimistic and pessimistic pictures of the future of the region are possible. What will be the future course of China, the most populous nation on the earth? How will the Soviet Union under Gorbachev behave toward this economically attractive region? What kind of economic and technological impact will Japan have on the region? Will Japan continue to remain a militarily small power? Will the United States be able to balance its concerns for the Atlantic and Pacific? How much will Canada be involved there, and will West Europe succeed in restoring an appropriate involvement and influence in the region? The region presents a challenge for all those desiring democratic values.

Trilateral Transactions with East Asia: A Statistical Appendix

Statistical Appendix

TABLE I-1

**Gross National Products and Average Annual Growth Rates
of Trilateral Countries and East Asia**
(in billion U.S. dollars)

	GNP (1982)	GNP PER CAPITA (1982)	AVERAGE ANNUAL GROWTH RATE (1978-82)
Japan	1,063.1	8,975	4.5%
Korea, Rep. of	68.2	1,734	6.7%
Taiwan	45.8	2,483	7.3%
Hong Kong	26	4,962	9.6%
China	297.4[1]	300[1]	5.0%[2]
Indonesia	90.2	575	6.8%
Philippines	38.9	785	5.4%
Thailand	37.3	770	6.5%
Malaysia	25.9	1,780	6.9%
Singapore	14.7	5,877	9.0%
U.S.	3,073.0	13,242	1.6%
Canada	298.1	12,010	1.6%
Germany, F.R.	658.9	10,690	1.6%
France	541.5	9,986	2.1%
UK	485.1	8,610	1.7%
Italy	344.4	6,070	1.7%
Spain	181.2	4,778	1.0%
Netherlands	137.6	9,615	0.6%
Sweden	99.2	11,904	1.4%
Switzerland	96.5	15,227	1.5%
Belgium	84.3	8,557	1.8%
Denmark	56.4	11,014	1.6%

Notes: (1) for 1981
(2) for 1960-81

TABLE I-2a
Growth in Defense Capabilities of Non-Communist East Asian Countries, 1974-75 and 1984-85

Year	Brunei 1974-75	Brunei 1984-85	Indonesia 1974-75	Indonesia 1984-85	Malaysia 1974-75	Malaysia 1984-85	Philippines 1974-75	Philippines 1984-85	Singapore 1974-75	Singapore 1984-85	Thailand 1974-75	Thailand 1984-85	Burma 1974-75	Burma 1984-85	Japan 1974-75	Japan 1984-85	South Korea 1974-75	South Korea 1984-85	Taiwan 1974-75	Taiwan 1984-85
Total Armed Forces		3,950	270,000	281,000	66,200	124,500	55,000	104,800	21,700	55,500	195,500	235,300	159,000	180,500	233,000	245,000	625,000	622,000	491,000	484,000
Defense Expenditures ($ U.S. million)		163	452	2,527	311	2,170	136	601	235	1,075	365	1,652	101	220	3,835	12,488	558	4,315	774	3,574
Missiles		SAM SSM	SSM	SAM SSM	SAM SSM	AAM SAM SSM	SAM	AAM	SAM	AAM SAM SSM	SAM	AAM SSM SAM			SSM SAM	AAM SSM SAM	SSM SAM	AAM SAM SSM	SAM	AAM ASM SSM SAM
Tanks — M&Md B.T.†			•									195			500	1,020	1,000	1,200	•	625
Tanks — Lt T.†		16		164		25	8	28	75	350	150	344	24		190				309	1,120
Naval Vessels — Destroyers			7	2											27	32	6	11	18	23
Naval Vessels — Frigates			5	9	2	2	7				7	6		1		18		8	2	9
Naval Vessels — SS†				3											14	14				2
Naval Vessels — SSBN†																				
Naval Vessels — SSN†																				
Combat Aircraft		6	106	100	36	34	82	36	65	167	105	203	11	38	495	351	210	440	206	547

Notes: • represents the presence of equipment where the exact number is not known

†M&Md B.T. = Medium and Main Battle Tanks
Lt T. = Light Tanks
SS = Diesel Submarines
SSBN = Ballistic-Missile Nuclear Submarines
SSN = Nuclear Submarines

Source: Compiled from the International Institute of Strategic Studies' *Military Balance 1974-75* and *1984-85*.

TABLE I-2b

Growth of Defense Capabilities of Other East Asian Countries, 1974-75 and 1984-85

YEAR		PRC		CAMBODIA		NORTH KOREA		LAOS		S. VIET.	N. VIET.	VIETNAM
		1974-75	1984-85	1974-75	1984-85	1974-75	1984-85	1974-75	1984-85	1974-75	1974-75	1984-85
Total Armed Forces		3,000,000	4,000,000	220,500	30,000	467,000	784,500	62,800	53,700	565,000	583,000	1,227,000
Defense Expenditure ($U.S. million)		4,500-10-12,000	8,190	98	N.A.	770	2,038	27	26	672	584	N.A.
Missiles		IRBM MRBM,SSM	AAM,ICBM IRBM,MRBM SAM,SSM			SAM,SSM	AAM SAM,SSM		AAM		AAM,SAM	AAM SAM,SSM
Tanks	M & Md B.T.†	*	11,450		*	900	2,675		30	600	900	1,900
	Lt T.†	*	*		*	130	150	10	25	600	*	600
Naval Vessels	Destroyers	7	14				4					
	Frigates		22				21			9		
	SS†	51	100			4						
	SSBN†		1									
	SSN†		2									
Combat Aircraft		4,500	6,100	64		598	740	81	20	509	203	290

Notes: * represents the presence of equipment where the exact number is not known

† M&Md B.T. = Medium and Main Battle Tanks
　Lt T. = Light Tanks
　SS = Diesel Submarines
　SSBN = Ballistic-Missile Nuclear Submarines
　SSN = Nuclear Submarines

Source: Compiled from the International Institute of Strategic Studies' *Military Balance 1974-75 and 1984-85.*

TABLE II-1a

Trilateral Trade with East Asia

(in million U.S. dollars)

from \ to	EAST ASIA[1]		JAPAN		U.S.		CANADA		WORLD	
	1977	1982	1977	1982	1977	1982	1977	1982	1977	1982
Western Europe[2]	8,805.6	18,011.8	4,497.3	7,908.3	28,025.8	48,383.4	4,215.1	5,390.0	457,638.0	709,481.2
	(0.2%)	(2.5%)	(1.0%)	(1.1%)	(6.1%)	(6.8%)	(0.9%)	(0.8%)	(100%)	(100%)
EEC	7,308.4	14,957.0	3,549.3	6,164.3	23,528.4	41,353.4	3,498.4	4,432.7	381,964.6	585,103.9
	(1.9%)	(2.6%)	(0.9%)	(1.1%)	(6.2%)	(7.1%)	(0.9%)	(0.8%)	(100%)	(100%)
Japan	15,504.8	28,751.8			19,929.4	36,640.9	1,707.8	2,860.7	80,494.8	138,831.2
	(19.3%)	(20.7%)			(24.8%)	(26.4%)	(2.1%)	(2.1%)	(100%)	(100%)
U.S.	7,687.8	20,104.0	10,419.4	20,366.8			25,008.8	32,415.0	117,926.4	207,160.2
	(6.5%)	(9.7%)	(8.8%)	(9.8%)			(21.2%)	(15.6%)	(100%)	(100%)
Canada	822.4	2,192.6	2,346.0	3,696.4	28,637.4	46,681.6			41,293.1	68,392.8
	(2.0%)	(3.2%)	(5.7%)	(5.4%)	(69.4%)	(68.3%)			(100%)	(100%)

Exports

Imports

from / to	EAST ASIA(1) 1977	EAST ASIA(1) 1982	JAPAN 1977	JAPAN 1982	U.S. 1977	U.S. 1982	CANADA 1977	CANADA 1982	WORLD 1977	WORLD 1982
Western Europe(2)	11,451.3 (2.3%)	19,011.6 (2.5%)	13,299.0 (2.7%)	23,403.4 (3.1%)	36,689.8 (7.5%)	63,564.6 (8.4%)	5,674.4 (1.2%)	7,558.9 (1.0%)	489,372.4 (100%)	760,200.4 (100%)
EEC	9,636.6 (2.5%)	16,226.3 (2.6%)	9,788.5 (2.5%)	17,885.1 (2.9%)	29,792.5 (7.6%)	50,684.0 (8.3%)	5,002.5 (1.3%)	6,563.4 (1.1%)	393,298.9 (100%)	613,488.1 (100%)
Japan	13,373.8 (18.9%)	31,560.7 (23.9%)			12,419.3 (17.5%)	24,227.3 (18.4%)	2,880.8 (4.1%)	4,440.5 (3.4%)	70,808.7 (100%)	131,931.2 (100%)
U.S.	13,276.3 (9.0%)	26,297.2 (10.3%)	18,900.4 (12.8%)	39,916.3 (15.7%)			29,757.5 (20.1%)	46,792.0 (18.4%)	147,862.4 (100%)	254,862.3 (100%)
Canada	853.7 (2.2%)	1,502.4 (2.7%)	1,695.0 (4.3%)	2,859.3 (5.2%)	27,796.6 (70.4%)	38,713.2 (70.6%)			39,484.8 (100%)	54,824.0 (100%)

Notes: (1) East Asia includes Burma, Hong Kong, Indonesia, South Korea, Malaysia, Philippines, Singapore, Thailand, Brunei, Laos, Kampuchea, Vietnam, PRC and North Korea.

(2) Western Europe includes Austria, Finland, Iceland, Norway, Portugal, Spain, Sweden and Switzerland as well as the ten EEC member countries.

Source: Compiled from the United Nations' *Commodity Trade Statistics*.

TABLE II-1b

Western Europe's Exports to East Asia in Comparison to the U.S. and Canada
(in million U.S. dollars)

	East Asia (1)		U.S.		Canada		World	
	1977	1982	1977	1982	1977	1982	1977	1982
Austria	146.1 (1.5%)	425.3 (2.7%)	305.9 (3.1%)	461.8 (3.0%)	66.6 (0.7%)	75.5 (0.5%)	9,807.7 (100.0%)	15,697.0 (100.0%)
Finland	127.2 (1.7%)	309.8 (2.4%)	339.6 (4.4%)	414.5 (3.2%)	42.8 (0.6%)	91.9 (0.7%)	7,668.9 (100.0%)	13,133.1 (100.0%)
Iceland	20.1 (3.9%)	24.7 (3.6%)	155.2 (30.3%)	176.8 (25.8%)	1.3 (0.3%)	3.6 (0.5%)	512.7 (100.0%)	684.9 (100.0%)
Sweden	512.2 (2.7%)	1,011.0 (3.8%)	1,023.7 (5.4%)	1,908.2 (7.1%)	225.0 (1.2%)	290.3 (1.1%)	19,054.4 (100.0%)	26,795.2 (100.0%)
Switzerland	1,031.2 (5.8%)	1,754.9 (6.7%)	1,172.8 (6.6%)	2,033.9 (7.8%)	195.2 (1.1%)	256.2 (1.0%)	17,681.6 (100.0%)	26,023.8 (100.0%)
Norway	375.0 (4.3%)	500.6 (2.8%)	361.2 (4.1%)	484.5 (2.8%)	58.2 (0.7%)	71.0 (0.4%)	8,717.2 (100.0%)	17,588.6 (100.0%)
Portugal	31.5 (1.6%)	69.6 (1.7%)	135.1 (6.7%)	257.6 (6.2%)	25.4 (1.3%)	34.3 (0.8%)	2,013.4 (100.0%)	4,171.0 (100.0%)
Spain	201.9 (2.0%)	703.1 (3.5%)	1,003.9 (9.8%)	1,293.2 (6.4%)	102.2 (1.0%)	134.2 (0.7%)	10,217.7 (100.0%)	20,283.7 (100.0%)
Belgium-Luxembourg	652.8 (1.7%)	1,395.5 (2.7%)	1,565.2 (4.2%)	2,305.9 (4.4%)	128.7 (0.3%)	200.1 (0.4%)	37,450.3 (100.0%)	52,398.0 (100.0%)
Denmark	308.9 (3.1%)	645.0 (4.3%)	559.6 (5.6%)	870.3 (5.8%)	73.5 (0.7%)	96.8 (0.6%)	9,912.8 (100.0%)	14,965.7 (100.0%)

COUNTRIES

Community

France	1,574.8 (2.5%)	3,582.3 (3.9%)	3,266.9 (5.2%)	5,245.8 (5.7%)	521.8 (0.8%)	706.9 (0.8%)	63,363.4 (100.0%)	92,622.7 (100.0%)
Germany	3,847.6 (3.3%)	7,047.7 (4.0%)	7,867.7 (6.7%)	11,590.7 (6.6%)	947.0 (0.8%)	1,045.0 (0.6%)	117,932.4 (100.0%)	176,247.5 (100.0%)
Greece (2)	38.3 (1.4%)	42.6 (1.0%)	128.0 (4.6%)	381.7 (8.3%)	24.3 (0.9%)	13.9 (0.3%)	2,757.3 (100.0%)	4,297.1 (100.0%)
Ireland	63.0 (1.4%)	170.3 (2.1%)	291.7 (6.6%)	576.8 (7.2%)	46.2 (1.0%)	140.5 (1.7%)	4,400.9 (100.0%)	8,061.9 (100.0%)
Italy	828.5 (1.8%)	2,102.1 (2.9%)	2,995.6 (6.6%)	5,179.7 (7.1%)	368.1 (0.8%)	557.6 (0.8%)	45,064.9 (100.0%)	73,445.9 (100.0%)
Netherlands	879.8 (2.0%)	1,267.3 (1.9%)	1,497.8 (3.4%)	2,153.1 (3.2%)	163.3 (0.4%)	185.3 (0.3%)	43,604.8 (100.0%)	66,404.0 (100.0%)
U.K.	2,664.3 (4.6%)	4,868.0 (5.0%)	5,355.8 (9.3%)	13,049.7 (13.5%)	1,225.1 (2.1%)	1,486.6 (1.5%)	57,477.7 (100.0%)	96,661.1 (100.0%)
Western Europe	13,302.9 (2.9%)	25,920.4 (3.7%)	28,025.8 (6.1%)	48,383.4 (6.8%)	4,215.1 (0.9%)	5,389.8 (0.8%)	457,638.0 (100.0%)	709,481.2 (100.0%)
U.S.	18,107.2 (15.4%)	40,470.8 (19.5%)	—	—	25,008.8 (21.2%)	32,415.0 (15.6%)	117,926.4 (100.0%)	207,160.2 (100.0%)
Canada	3,168.4 (7.7%)	5,889.0 (8.6%)	28,637.4 (69.4%)	46,681.6 (68.3%)	—	—	41,293.1 (100.0%)	68,392.8 (100.0%)

European Economic Commission

TRILATERAL COMMISSION

Notes: (1) East Asia includes Brunei, Burma, China, Hong Kong, Indonesia, Japan, Malaysia, North Korea, Philippines, Singapore, South Korea, Thailand, and Vietnam.
(2) Greece is not a member country of the Trilateral Commission as of March 1985.

Source: The United Nations' *Commodity Trade Statistics*.

TABLE II-1c

Western Europe's Imports from East Asia in Comparison to the U.S. and Canada
(in million U.S. dollars)

		East Asia (1)		U.S.		Canada		World	
		1977	1982	1977	1982	1977	1982	1977	1982
	Austria	493.6 (3.5%)	852.9 (4.4%)	425.1 (3.0%)	736.5 (3.8%)	55.9 (0.4%)	88.7 (0.5%)	14,247.8 (100.0%)	19,548.3 (100.0%)
	Finland	289.8 (3.8%)	746.4 (5.6%)	356.3 (4.7%)	818.0 (6.1%)	21.0 (0.3%)	118.5 (0.9%)	7,612.0 (100.0%)	13,388.6 (100.0%)
	Iceland	26.4 (4.3%)	56.2 (6.0%)	40.0 (6.6%)	79.5 (8.4%)	1.8 (0.3%)	5.4 (0.6%)	607.1 (100.0%)	941.7 (100.0%)
	Sweden	1,320.8 (6.6%)	1,671.7 (6.1%)	1,437.6 (7.1%)	2,352.7 (8.5%)	114.5 (0.6%)	182.2 (0.7%)	20,140.2 (100.0%)	27,543.6 (100.0%)
	Switzerland	889.2 (4.9%)	1,684.6 (5.9%)	1,209.5 (6.7%)	2,060.1 (7.2%)	103.4 (0.6%)	142.5 (0.5%)	17,979.4 (100.0%)	28,670.0 (100.0%)
	Norway	1,131.2 (8.8%)	1,372.6 (8.9%)	787.1 (6.1%)	1,419.3 (9.2%)	189.2 (1.5%)	210.0 (1.4%)	12,874.9 (100.0%)	15,476.7 (100.0%)
	Portugal	260.7 (5.3%)	410.6 (4.3%)	505.8 (10.2%)	1,038.0 (10.8%)	33.1 (0.7%)	59.8 (0.6%)	4,964.0 (100.0%)	9,606.5 (100.0%)
	Spain	913.5 (5.2%)	1,508.6 (4.8%)	2,136.1 (12.1%)	4,377.0 (13.9%)	153.2 (0.9%)	188.2 (0.6%)	17,648.0 (100.0%)	31,536.8 (100.0%)
Community	Belgium-Luxembourg	1,117.4 (2.8%)	1,894.7 (3.3%)	2,426.2 (6.0%)	4,073.5 (7.0%)	329.8 (0.8%)	407.4 (0.7%)	40,140.2 (100.0%)	57,926.7 (100.0%)
COUNTRIES	Denmark	758.1 (5.7%)	882.2 (5.2%)	756.5 (5.7%)	1,002.3 (6.0%)	46.9 (0.4%)	61.0 (0.4%)	13,239.7 (100.0%)	16,840.1 (100.0%)

European Economic Commission	France	2,577.6 (3.7%)	5,298.1 (4.6%)	4,890.2 (7.0%)	9,117.6 (7.9%)	534.5 (0.8%)	803.5 (0.7%)	70,275.8 (100.0%)	115,628.7 (100.0%)
	Germany	6,070.3 (6.0%)	10,435.2 (6.7%)	7,312.9 (7.3%)	11,641.8 (7.5%)	1,008.9 (1.0%)	1,361.5 (0.9%)	100,700.9 (100.0%)	155,155.3 (100.0%)
	Greece (2)	1,091.1 (15.9%)	791.6 (7.9%)	350.1 (5.1%)	423.7 (4.2%)	27.9 (0.4%)	45.3 (0.5%)	6,852.5 (100.0%)	10,022.8 (100.0%)
	Ireland	187.8 (3.5%)	443.1 (4.6%)	477.3 (8.9%)	1,247.7 (12.9%)	61.2 (1.1%)	135.3 (1.4%)	5,384.8 (100.0%)	9,700.4 (100.0%)
	Italy	1,438.1 (3.0%)	2,629.4 (3.0%)	3,285.3 (6.9%)	5,834.0 (6.8%)	544.8 (1.1%)	740.8 (0.9%)	47,580.7 (100.0%)	86,229.2 (100.0%)
	Netherlands	2,276.2 (5.0%)	3,378.8 (5.4%)	3,876.1 (8.5%)	5,738.6 (9.2%)	337.3 (0.7%)	501.2 (0.8%)	45,500.0 (100.0%)	62,583.2 (100.0%)
	U.K.	3,908.3 (6.1%)	8,358.4 (8.4%)	6,418.0 (10.1%)	11,604.7 (11.7%)	2,111.2 (3.3%)	2,507.5 (2.5%)	63,624.8 (100.0%)	99,401.8 (100.0%)
TRILATERAL	Western Europe	24,750.3 (5.4%)	42,415.0 (6.0%)	30,690.0 (7.5%)	63,564.6 (8.4%)	5,674.4 (1.2%)	7,558.9 (1.0%)	489,372.4 (100.0%)	760,200.4 (100.0%)
	U.S.	32,176.7 (21.8%)	66,213.5 (26.0%)	—	—	29,757.5 (20.1%)	46,792.0 (18.4%)	147,862.4 (100.0%)	254,862.3 (100.0%)
	Canada	2,548.7 (6.5%)	4,361.7 (8.0%)	27,796.6 (70.4%)	38,713.2 (70.6%)	—	—	39,484.8 (100.0%)	54,824.0 (100.0%)

Notes: (1) East Asia includes Brunei, Burma, China, Hong Kong, Indonesia, Japan, Malaysia, North Korea, Philippines, Singapore, South Korea, Thailand, and Vietnam.
(2) Greece is not a member country of the Trilateral Commission as of March 1985.

Source: The United Nations' *Commodity Trade Statistics*.

TABLE II-1d

EEC Trade with ASEAN in 1982
(in million U.S. dollars)

	Exports to			Imports from		
	I ASEAN	II WORLD	I/II (%)	I ASEAN	II WORLD	I/II (%)
Belgium-Luxembourg	392.1	52,398.0	0.7%	342.3	57,926.7	0.6%
Denmark	180.9	14,965.7	1.2%	150.5	16,840.0	0.9%
France	1,614.1	92,622.7	1.7%	1,112.3	115,628.7	1.0%
Germany	2,880.8	176,247.5	1.6%	2,097.6	155,155.3	1.4%
Greece	3.4	4,297.1	0.0%	99.7	10,022.8	1.0%
Ireland	47.9	8,061.9	0.6%	76.5	9,700.4	0.8%
Italy	644.9	73,445.9	0.9%	704.5	86,229.2	0.8%
Netherlands	631.1	66,404.0	1.0%	1,291.5	62,583.2	2.1%
U.K.	1,798.6	96,661.1	1.9%	1,270.6	99,401.8	1.3%
EEC Total	8,193.8	585,103.9	1.4%	7,145.5	613,488.1	1.2%

Source: Compiled from the United Nations' *Commodity Trade Statistics*.

TABLE II-1e

ASEAN Trade with the Trilateral Countries
(in millions U.S. dollars)

	ASEAN EXPORTS TO		ASEAN IMPORTS FROM	
	1977	1982	1977	1982
Japan	7,801.3	20,391.6	7,161.5	16,250.6
	(24.5%)	(29.1%)	(23.8%)	(21.6%)
U.S.	6,846.9	10,211.8	4,107.2	11,316.6
	(21.5%)	(14.6%)	(13.6%)	(15.1%)
Canada	216.9	378.8	331.0	591.1
	(0.7%)	(0.5%)	(1.1%)	(0.8%)
Western Europe	5,157.4	7,768.5	5,003.5	10,771.7
	(16.2%)	(11.1%)	(16.6%)	(14.3%)
EEC	4,586.0	7,101.5	4,370.2	9,047.5
	(14.4%)	(10.1%)	(14.5%)	(12.0%)
Others	11,769.2	31,341.3	13,498.0	36,167.9
	(37.0%)	(44.7%)	(44.8%)	(48.2%)
Total	31,791.7	70,092.0	30,101.2	75,097.9
	(100%)	(100%)	(100%)	(100%)

Source: Compiled from the United Nations' *Commodity Trade Statistics*

TABLE II-1f

East Asian Trade with Trilateral Countries in 1977 and 1982
(in million U.S. dollars)

		Exports								
		WESTERN EUROPE		JAPAN		NORTH AMERICA		WORLD		
from \ to		1977	1982	1977	1982	1977	1982	1977	1982	
Brunei	(1)	1.4 (0.1%)	27.0 (0.9%)	1,245.8 (76.5%)	2,390.3 (75.4%)	149.1 (9.2%)	275.8 (8.7%)	1,628.0 (100%)	3,170.6 (100%)	
Burma	(2)	39.5 (19.2%)	73.0 (18.7%)	14.0 (6.9%)	44.3 (11.4%)	2.0 (1.0%)	21.8 (5.6%)	206.2 (100%)	389.8 (100%)	
Hong Kong	(3)	2,527.0 (26.3%)	4,419.6 (21.1%)	585.1 (6.1%)	945.0 (4.5%)	3,497.4 (36.3%)	6,857.4 (32.7%)	9,626.1 (100%)	20,984.7 (100%)	
Indonesia	(4)	968.5 (8.9%)	917.5 (4.1%)	4,360.8 (40.2%)	11,192.6 (50.2%)	3,591.2 (33.1%)	4,490.9 (20.1%)	10,852.6 (100%)	22,293.3 (100%)	
Kampuchea	(5)	—	—	—	—	—	—	—	—	
Korea, Rep. of	(6)	1,754.5 (17.5%)	3,740.7 (17.1%)	2,148.3 (21.4%)	3,388.1 (15.5%)	3,534.6 (35.2%)	7,261.6 (33.2%)	10,046.4 (100%)	21,853.4 (100%)	
Laos	(7)	0.1 (0.6%)	0.9 (3.8%)	2.3 (13.9%)	1.1 (4.6%)	0.9 (5.5%)	1.4 (5.9%)	16.5 (100%)	23.9 (100%)	

Malaysia	(8)	1,345.0 (22.1%)	1,951.4 (16.2%)	1,244.9 (20.5%)	2,449.1 (20.3%)	1,169.8 (19.2%)	1,471.1 (12.2%)	6,083.8 (100%)	12,043.5 (100%)
Philippines	(9)	645.0 (20.5%)	929.8 (18.6%)	731.7 (23.2%)	1,145.1 (22.9%)	1,151.1 (36.5%)	1,671.3 (33.4%)	3,150.9 (100%)	5,010.2 (100%)
Singapore	(10)	1,397.9 (17.0%)	2,225.1 (10.7%)	786.8 (9.5%)	2,263.2 (10.9%)	1,496.8 (18.2%)	3,086.4 (14.8%)	8,240.8 (100%)	20,787.9 (100%)
Taiwan*	(11)	1,255 (13.4%)	1,316 (5.9%)	1,120 (12.0%)	2,378 (10.7%)	3,912 (41.8%)	9,269 (41.7%)	9,361 (100%)	22,204 (100%)
Thailand	(12)	832.3 (23.9%)	1,828.6 (26.0%)	686.0 (19.7%)	954.9 (13.6%)	355.0 (10.2%)	902.8 (12.8%)	3,481.6 (100%)	7,040.1 (100%)
Vietnam	(13)	10.5 (7.9%)	12.1 (6.4%)	48.4 (36.5%)	32.7 (17.4%)	0.5 (0.4%)	0.1 (0.1%)	132.6 (100%)	188.3 (100%)
Total		10,776.7	17,441.7	11,334.3	27,184.4	18,860.4	35,309.6	62,825.9	135,989.7
Percent of World Total		17.2%	12.3%	18.0%	20.0%	30.0%	26.0%		

*Based on *Key Indicators of Developing Member Countries of ADB* (Manila: Economic Office, Asian Development Bank, April 1984).
Source: Compiled from the United Nations' *Statistical Yearbook of Asia and the Pacific*

TABLE II-1f (continued)

East Asian Trade with Trilateral Countries in 1977 and 1982
(in million U.S. dollars)

from / to		WESTERN EUROPE		JAPAN		Imports NORTH AMERICA		WORLD	
		1977	1982	1977	1982	1977	1982	1977	1982
Brunei	(1)	61.4 (22.2%)	125.5 (14.3%)	59.2 (21.4%)	158.3 (18.1%)	58.5 (21.2%)	86.8 (1.0%)	276.4 (100%)	874.6 (100%)
Burma	(2)	75.7 (27.7%)	318.4 (36.9%)	64.9 (23.8%)	253.7 (29.4%)	14.7 (5.4%)	41.5 (4.8%)	273.1 (100%)	863.0 (100%)
Hong Kong	(3)	1,712.0 (16.4%)	3,456.6 (14.7%)	2,479.5 (23.7%)	5,198.1 (22.1%)	1,406.8 (13.5%)	2,760.6 (11.7%)	10,457.6 (100%)	23,553.5 (100%)
Indonesia	(4)	1,401.6 (22.5%)	3,254.6 (19.3%)	1,689.0 (27.1%)	4,278.5 (25.5%)	879.8 (14.1%)	2,578.9 (15.3%)	6,203.3 (100%)	16,858.9 (100%)
Kampuchea	(5)								
Korea, Rep. of	(6)	984.5 (9.1%)	2,126.1 (8.8%)	3,926.6 (36.3%)	5,305.3 (21.9%)	2,620.7 (24.2%)	6,732.3 (27.8%)	10,810.5 (100%)	24,250.8 (100%)
Laos	(7)	12.3 (20.4%)	14.7 (17.8%)	16.0 (26.5%)	10.7 (12.9%)	—	0.4 (0.0%)	60.3 (100%)	82.8 (100%)

Malaysia	(8)	884.2 (19.4%)	1,759.1 (14.2%)	1,065.0 (23.4%)	3,101.4 (25.0%)	616.7 (13.6%)	2,340.5 (18.9%)	4,546.7 (100%)	12,408.9 (100%)
Philippines	(9)	535.9 (13.7%)	1,049.7 (12.6%)	975.3 (24.9%)	1,645.1 (20.0%)	871.8 (22.3%)	2,036.7 (24.8%)	3,914.8 (100%)	8,229.0 (100%)
Singapore	(10)	1,361.8 (13.0%)	3,530.8 (12.5%)	1,835.5 (17.5%)	5,044.0 (17.9%)	1,384.2 (13.2%)	3,847.8 (13.7%)	10,470.6 (100%)	28,166.8 (100%)
Taiwan*	(11)	453 (5.3%)	2,116 (11.2%)	2,643 (30.7%)	4,780 (25.3%)	2,037 (23.7%)	4,879 (25.8%)	8,605 (100%)	18,888 (100%)
Thailand	(12)	828.5 (17.9%)	1,166.8 (13.1%)	1,500.9 (35.4%)	2,216.2 (24.8%)	659.9 (14.2%)	1,193.6 (13.4%)	4,639.2 (100%)	8,939.5 (100%)
Vietnam	(13)	226.1 (33.6%)	114.7 (18.0%)	159.7 (23.8%)	101.4 (15.9%)	11.5 (1.7%)	35.6 (5.6%)	672.3 (100%)	636.7 (100%)
Total		8,537.0	19,033.0	16,414.6	32,092.7	10,561.6	26,533.7	60,956.8	143,752.5
Percent of World Total		14.0%	13.2%	26.9%	22.3%	17.3%	18.5%		

*Based on *Key Indicators of Developing Member Countries of ADB* (Manila: Economic Office, Asian Development Bank, April 1984).
Source: Compiled from the United Nations' *Statistical Yearbook of Asia and the Pacific*

TABLE II-2a

Estimated Stock of DAC Direct Investment in Developing Countries at Year-end 1978 and 1981 by Host Region
(in billion U.S. dollars)

	END 1978	END 1981
Europe	8.17 (9.1%)	11.5 (8.4%)
Africa	6.59 (7.4%)	15.5 (11.3%)
Latin America	50.33 (56.4%)	71.8 (52.3%)
Middle East	1.22 (1.4%)	
Asia	23.00[1] (25.8%)	38.4[2] (28.0%)
Total	89.31 (100%)	137.2 (100%)

Notes: (1) Includes Oceania. Stock in East/Southeast Asia as defined in this report (Brunei, Burma, Hong Kong, Indonesia, ROK, Malaysia, Philippines, Singapore, Taiwan and Thailand) amounts to $U.S. 18.42 billion or 20.6% of the Total.
(2) Since 16% of the $137.2 billion total went to OPEC countries, this figure must include some Middle East countries.

Source: Compiled from the OECD, *Recent International Direct Investment Trends* (Paris, 1981) and *Investing in Developing Countries* (Fifth Revised Edition, Paris, 1983).

TABLE II-2b

Distribution of Geographically Allocated Direct Investment Flows (Net) from Major Source Countries, 1979-81[1]
(in percent)

SOURCE COUNTRY	EUROPE	AFRICA	LATIN AMERICA	ASIA	TOTAL
France	33 (34)	23 (16)	39 (6)	5 (2)	100
Germany	21 (18)	5 (3)	59 (7)	15 (4)	100
Japan	1 (4)	9 (16)	29 (11)	61 (49)	100
U.K.[2]	10 (13)	30 (25)	36 (7)	24 (9)	100
U.S.	5 (31)	9 (40)	69 (69)	17 (36)	100
Total	(100)	(100)	(100)	(100)	

Notes: (1) Figures in parentheses indicate percentage share of total foreign direct investment by five source countries to the region. They also include official Japanese government support for private investment.
(2) Figures exclude investments in the oil industry.

Source: OECD, *Investing in Developing Countries* (Fifth Revised Edition, Paris 1983)

TABLE II-2c
Japanese Direct Overseas Investment Outflow by Region
(register/approved basis, in million U.S. dollars)

	1977	1978	1979	1980	1981	1982	1983
North America	735	1,364	1,438	1,596	2,497	2,905	2,701
	(26.2%)	(29.7%)	(28.8%)	(34.0%)	(28.0%)	(37.7%)	(33.2%)
Latin America	456	616	1,207	588	1,181	1,503	1,878
	(16.3%)	(13.4%)	(24.2%)	(12.5%)	(13.3%)	(19.5%)	(23.1%)
Asia	865	1,340	976	1,186	3,338	1,384	1,847
	(30.8%)	(29.1%)	(19.5%)	(25.3%)	(37.5%)	(18.0%)	(22.7%)
Hong Kong	109	159	225	156	329	400	563
Indonesia	425	610	150	529	2,434	410	374
ROK	95	222	95	35	73	103	129
Malaysia	69	48	33	146	31	83	140
Philippines	27	53	102	78	72	34	65
Singapore	66	174	225	140	226	180	322
Taiwan	18	40	39	47	54	55	103
Thailand	49	32	55	33	31	94	72
Others	7	2	22	21	48	25	81
Middle East	225	492	130	158	96	124	175
	(8.0%)	(10.7%)	(2.6%)	(3.4%)	(1.1%)	(1.6%)	(2.1%)
Europe	220	323	495	578	798	876	990
	(7.8%)	(7.0%)	(9.9%)	(12.3%)	(9.0%)	(11.4%)	(12.2%)
Africa	140	225	168	139	573	489	364
	(5.0%)	(4.9%)	(3.4%)	(3.0%)	(6.4%)	(6.3%)	(4.5%)
Oceania	165	239	582	448	424	421	191
	(5.9%)	(5.2%)	(11.6%)	(9.5%)	(4.8%)	(5.5%)	(2.3%)
Total	2,806	4,598	4,995	4,693	8,906	7,703	8,145
	(100%)	(100%)	(100%)	(100%)	(100%)	(100%)	(100%)

Source: Compiled from *Kaigai Toshi Kenkyu-sho Ho* (Bulletin of Institute of Overseas Investment, Export-Import Bank of Japan), Vol. 4. no. 9; Vol. 5. no. 10; Vol. 6. no. 9; Vol. 7. no. 9; Vol. 8. no. 10; Vol. 9. no. 10; and Vol 10. no. 10.

TABLE II-2d

U.S. Direct Investment Abroad at Year-end 1972-1982 by Recipient Region
(in million U.S. dollars)

	1972	1973	1974	1975	1976	1977	1978	1979	1980	1981	1982
Canada	25,771 (27.3%)	25,541 (24.6%)	28,404 (23.9%)	31,038 (24.9%)	33,932 (24.9%)	35,200 (23.5%)	37,071 (22.1%)	40,243 (21.4%)	44,978 (20.9%)	45,129 (19.9%)	44,509 (20.1%)
Europe	30,817 (32.7%)	38,225 (36.9%)	44,782 (37.7%)	49,533 (39.9%)	55,139 (40.4%)	60,930 (40.7%)	69,553 (41.4%)	82,622 (44.0%)	96,539 (44.8%)	101,514 (44.8%)	99,877 (45.1%)
Japan	2,375 (2.5%)	2,671 (2.6%)	3,319 (2.8%)	3,339 (2.7%)	3,797 (2.9%)	4,143 (2.8%)	4,972 (3.0%)	6,208 (3.3%)	6,243 (2.9%)	6,755 (3.0%)	6,872 (3.1%)
Other Developed Countries (f)	5,395 (5.7%)	5,746 (5.5%)	6,520 (5.5%)	7,013 (5.6%)	7,530 (5.5%)	7,952 (5.3%)	8,876 (5.3%)	9,595 (5.1%)	10,590 (4.9%)	11,998 (5.3%)	11,818 (5.3%)
Latin America	16,796 (17.8%)	16,484 (15.9%)	19,491 (16.4%)	22,101 (17.8%)	23,934 (17.5%)	28,110 (18.8%)	32,662 (19.5%)	35,056 (18.7%)	38,882 (18.0%)	38,864 (17.2%)	33,039 (14.9%)
Africa	3,091 (3.3%)	2,376 (2.3%)	2,233 (1.9%)	2,414 (1.9%)	2,775 (2.0%)	2,802 (1.9%)	3,175 (1.9%)	3,028 (1.6%)	3,778 (1.8%)	4,228 (1.9%)	5,069 (2.3%)
Middle East	1,992 (2.1%)	2,588 (2.5%)	2,215 (1.9%)	-4,040 (-3.3%)	-3,730 (-2.7%)	-2,667 (-1.8%)	-2,194 (-1.3%)	-999 (-0.5%)	2,113 (1.0%)	1,992 (0.9%)	2,703 (1.2%)
Asia and Pacific	3,354 (3.6%)	3,818 (3.7%)	4,519 (3.8%)	5,747 (4.6%)	5,904 (4.3%)	6,217 (4.1%)	6,757 (4.0%)	7,440 (4.0%)	8,505 (3.9%)	11,099 (4.9%)	12,347 (5.6%)
International	4,743 (5.0%)	6,196 (6.0%)	7,335 (6.2%)	7,067 (5.7%)	7,114 (5.2%)	7,160 (4.8%)	6,934 (4.1%)	3,567 (1.9%)	3,951 (1.8%)	4,780 (2.1%)	5,110 (2.3%)
Total	94,337 (100%)	103,676 (100%)	118,819 (100%)	124,212 (100%)	136,396 (100%)	149,848 (100%)	167,804 (100%)	186,760 (100%)	215,578 (100%)	226,359 (100%)	221,343 (100%)

Note: (1) Includes Australia, New Zealand and South Africa.
Source: U.S. Department of Commerce, Survey of Current Business.

TABLE II-2e

British Net Overseas Investment Flows Analyzed by Area [1]
(in million U.S. dollars)

	1973	1978	1982 [2]
Western Europe	1,446.8 (38.5%)	1,736.3 (31.2%)	374.4 (8.5%)
North America	1,184.8 (31.5%)	2,247.6 (40.4%)	2,722.3 (61.5%)
Japan	18.1 (0.5%)	67.8 (1.2%)	24.0 (0.5%)
Other Developed Countries [3]	641.5 (17.1%)	578.1 (10.4%)	722.9 (16.3%)
Africa	147.6 (3.9%)	227.9 (5.0%)	458.9 (10.4%)
Middle East	25.3 (0.7%)	136.2 (2.4%)	75.4 (1.7%)
Asia	113.2 (3.0%)	61.5 (1.1%)	−504.0 (−11.4%)
Latin America	138.5 (3.7%)	423.1 (7.6%)	554.6 (12.5%)
Others	45.5 (1.2%)	21.1 (0.4%)	−4.5 (−0.1%)
World Total	3,760.3 (100%)	5,562.2 (100%)	4,424.5 (100%)

Notes: (1) Excludes oil companies.
    (2) According to the British Department of Trade and Industry, Asia in 1983, excluding Japan, received $676.4 million or 12.6% of the total outward investment of $5,363.4 million. Japan received $38.1 million or 0.7%.
    (3) "Other Developed Countries" includes Australia, New Zealand and South Africa.

Sources: Compiled from the British Department of Trade and Industry's *Business Monitor MA 4, Overseas Transactions* (1978 and 1982).

TABLE II-2f

Outward Flow of French Direct Foreign Investment by Region
(in million U.S. dollars)

	1978	1983
EEC	859.2 (33.9%)	402.2 (21.8%)
U.S.	387.6 (15.3%)	514.3 (27.8%)
Canada	92.7 (3.7%)	70.3 (3.8%)
Other OECD Members	576.5 (22.7%)	453.8 (24.6%)
Centrally Planned Economies	6.2 (0.2%)	5.9 (0.3%)
Latin America	241.5 (9.5%)	68.9[2] (3.7%)
International Organizations	—	13.6 (0.7%)
Others	372.9 (14.7%)	319.4 (17.3%)
Total	2,536.6[1] (100%)	1,848.4 (100%)

Notes: (1) Excludes French overseas territories.
(2) Includes only Argentina, Brazil and Mexico.

Source: *Balance des Paiements* (1978, Ministere de l'Economie) and *La Balance des Paiements de la France* (1983, Ministere de l'Economie).

TABLE II-2g

Outward Flow of German Direct Foreign Investment by Region
(in million U.S. dollars)

	1973	1978	1983
Europe	1,473.7 (69.8%)	1,358.5 (45.1%)	1,115.4 (36.3%)
U.S.	135.8 (6.4%)	938.2 (32.7%)	1,078.0 (35.1%)
Canada	122.5 (5.8%)	202.8 (6.7%)	−5.6 (−0.2%)
Latin America	137.4 (6.5%)	325.1 (10.8%)	454.0 (14.8%)
Africa	127.6 (6.0%)	20.9 (0.7%)	252.2 (8.2%)
Asia	113.8 (5.4%)	147.6 (4.9%)	131.0 (4.3%)
Oceania	0.9 (0.0%)	17.2 (0.6%)	48.5 (1.6%)
Total	2,111.6 (100%)	3,010.1 (100%)	3,073.6 (100%)

Source: *Leistung in Zahlen* (1983, Bundesministerium fur Wirtschaft), p. 79.

TABLE II-2h

Direct Foreign Investment to East and Southeast Asia
(in million U.S. dollars)

	JAPAN		U.S.		EUROPE		WORLD TOTAL	
	1977	1982	1977	1982	1977	1982	1977	1982
PRC[1]		7.5 (5.4%)		52.0 (37.0%)		14.3[4] (10.2%)		140.6 (100.0%)
Hong Kong[1]	84.4 (19.9%)	347.7 (30.1%)	197.4 (46.5%)	538.2 (46.6%)	83.5[5] (19.7%)	170.7[5] (14.8%)	424.4 (100.0%)	1,154.2 (100.0%)
Indonesia[2]	2,079.5[6] (38.7%)	4,343.7 (36.9%)	1,020.1 (19.0%)	663.7 (5.6%)	652.2 (12.1%)	1,379.3 (11.7%)	5,371.5 (100.0%)	11,777.3 (100.0%)
ROK[3]	26.7 (40.5%)	32.3 (27.2%)	14.6 (22.1%)	74.1 (62.4%)	12.5[8] (19.0%)	5.9[8] (5.0%)	65.9 (100.0%)	118.7 (100.0%)
Malaysia[1]	132.0 (20.0%)	239.6 (16.0%)	68.5 (10.4%)	82.5 (5.5%)	159.7[9] (24.2%)	388.8 (26.0%)	659.2 (100.0%)	1,497.1 (100.0%)
Philippines[2]	143.5 (25.3%)	402.0 (18.0%)	187.8 (33.1%)	1,077.0 (48.3%)	82.0[10] (14.5%)	219.0[10] (9.8%)	567.0 (100.0%)	2,228.0 (100.0%)
Singapore[3]	129.4 (35.7%)	94.2 (8.1%)	153.5 (42.3%)	513.7 (44.3%)	47.7[11] (13.2%)	402.7[11] (34.7%)	362.6 (100.0%)	1,160.5 (100.0%)

Taiwan[3]	24.2 (25.4%)	64.6[12] (18.1%)	24.2 (25.4%)	203.2[12] (57.0%)	28.0 (29.4%)	12.6[12] (3.5%)	95.2 (100.0%)	356.3[12] (100.0%)
Thailand[3]	39.4 (37.1%)	44.2 (23.6%)	24.1 (22.7%)	36.7 (19.6%)	23.4[13] (22.1%)	69.1[13] (36.9%)	106.1 (100.0%)	187.1 (100.0%)

Notes: (1) Year-end stock.
(2) Year-end accumulated flows.
(3) Annual flows.
(4) Includes only Denmark, France, Germany, Norway, Sweden, and Switzerland.
(5) Includes only France, Germany, Netherlands, Switzerland, and the U.K.
(6) As of June, 1978.
(7) Includes Germany, Netherlands, Switzerland, the U.K., and other unidentified European countries.
(8) Includes Austria, Belgium, France, Germany, Italy, Liechtenstein, Luxembourg, Netherlands, Spain, Switzerland, and the U.K.
(9) Includes Austria, Belgium, Denmark, France, Germany, Italy, Netherlands, Norway, Switzerland, Sweden, and the U.K.
(10) Includes only France, Germany, Switzerland, and the U.K.
(11) Includes France, Germany, Italy, Netherlands, Sweden, Switzerland, the U.K., and other unidentified European countries.
(12) Figures for 1981.
(13) Includes France, Germany, Italy, Netherlands, Switzerland, and the U.K.

Sources: Compiled from *Chugoku Keizai Nenkan* (Economic Yearbook of China), 1983; statistics released by the Colonial Government of Hong Kong and BKMP of Indonesia; Papua New Guinea's *Statistical Bulletin* (1976/77); Board of Investment and the Central Bank of the Philippines statistics; *EDB Annual Report* (1982) of Singapore; *Taiwan Statistical Data Book* (1982); and *Investment Report by Countries by* Thailand's Board of Investment reproduced in *Hatten Tojokoku ni Okeru Kaigai Toshi Tokei* (Overseas Investment Statistics of LDCs) (Tokyo: Institute of Developing Economies, 1984) and *Kaigai Shijo Hakusho—Toshi-hen* (Whitepaper on Overseas Markets—Investment Markets) (Tokyo: Japan External Trade Organization, 1977, '78, '79, '80, '81, '82, '83, and '84). For figures for Malaysia, statistics of the Malaysia Industrial Development Authority were used.

TABLE II-3

ODA Disbursements to East Asia
(in million U.S. dollars)

	Japan		U.S.		Canada		Western Europe[1]		Total ODA received from DAC countries	
	1977	1982	1977	1982	1977	1982	1977	1982	1977	1982
East Asia[2] (I)	379.3 (27.6%)	1,167.4 (46.5%)	258.0 (18.7%)	140.0 (5.6%)	24.8 (1.8%)	46.6 (1.9%)	407.2 (29.6%)	775.8 (30.9%)	1,376.6 (100%)	2,512.6 (100%)
Total (II)	899.3	2,367.3	2,897.0	4,861.0	475.4	826.7	5,418.3	10,789.5	10,080.5	18,432.5
(I)/(II) (%)	42.2%	49.3%	8.9%	2.9%	5.2%	5.6%	7.5%	7.2%	13.7%	13.6%

Notes: (1) Western Europe includes Austria, Belgium, Denmark, Finland, France, Germany, Italy, the Netherlands, Norway, Sweden, Switzerland and the U.K.
(2) East Asia includes Burma, China, Hong Kong, Indonesia, Kampuchea, Korea, Laos, Malaysia, Philippines, Singapore, Taiwan, Thailand and Vietnam.

Source: Compiled from the OECD's *Geographical Distribution of Financial Flows to Developing Countries.*

TABLE III-1

Number of Major Trilateral Countries' Diplomatic Representatives[1] in East Asia
(as of January 1985)

	France	Germany[2]	Italy[2]	U.K.	Japan	U.S.[3]	Canada
China	19	2	3	48	52	101	15
Hong Kong	6	2	2	x	24	77	28
Japan	20	9	4	47	x	97	35
ROK	8	2	3	22	41	91	11
Brunei	n.a.	1	1	5	8	n.a.	4
Indonesia	10	3	5	23	40	160	14
Malaysia	8	3	2	22	25	47	8
Philippines	10	1	2	14	31	321	16
Singapore	9	1	1	22	24	53	15
Thailand	13	1	2	30	48	124	19
Burma	5	1	2	11	16	38	4
Kampuchea	n.a.	n.a.	1	0	0	n.a.	n.a.
Laos	4	1	n.a.	4	10	9	3
Vietnam	8	1	1	7	11	n.a.	3

Notes: (1) Definition of diplomatic representative varies from country to country. The reporter tries to include diplomats working in chancery and press office, military attaches, economic and financial departments, scientific and cultural departments, and consular division and to exclude all the other officials or quasi-officials with no diplomatic status.

(2) German and Italian figures concern only ambassadors, consul generals, and consuls, excluding all other diplomatic staff. Economic and trade officers are not considered "diplomatic representation" by these countries. No other official figures are available.

(3) U.S. figures exclude federal civilian employees employed by army, navy, airforce and other military agencies in respective countries. Figures, therefore, represent number of representatives from the State Department, Department of Commerce, United States Information Agency (U.S.I.A.) and other civilian agencies on December 31,1982.

TABLE III-2

Trilateral Country Tourists in East and Southeast Asia

		Japan	U.S.	Western Europe	Total
Burma	1977	1,874 (8.5%)	3,008 (13.6%)	8,225[1] (37.3%)	22,076 (100%)
	1982				30,563 (100%)
Hong Kong	1977	485,500 (27.7%)	254,200 (14.5%)	71,100[2] (4.0%)	1,755,700 (100%)
	1981	508,000 (20.0%)	372,100 (14.7%)	167,100[2] (6.6%)	2,535,200 (100%)
Indonesia	1977	54,000 (11.7%)	57,300 (12.4%)	93,200[3] (20.1%)	463,000 (100%)
	1982	70,000 (11.7%)	52,300 (8.3%)	147,500[4] (24.7%)	598,100 (100%)
Kampuchea[5]					
South Korea	1977	581,500 (61.2%)	113,700 (12.0%)	28,300[6] (3.0%)	949,700 (100%)
	1980	468,400 (48.0%)	121,400 (12.4%)	12,400[2] (1.3%)	·976,400 (100%)
Malaysia	1977	111,000 (8.7%)	76,100 (6.0%)	83,500[2] (6.5%)	1,278,000 (100%)
	1979	101,700 (7.3%)	72,300 (5.2%)	85,500[2] (6.1%)	1,401,300 (100%)
Papua New Guinea	1977	1,467 (5.4%)	2,684 (10.0%)	878[7] (3.2%)	27,089 (100.0%)
	1981	2,260 (6.4%)	3,033 (8.6%)	1,419[8] (4.0%)	35,116 (100%)
Philippines	1977	213,200 (29.2%)	92,200 (12.6%)	93,300[9] (12.8%)	730,100 (100%)
	1982	159,918 (18.0%)	177,627 (20.0%)	110,109[10] (12.4%)	890,807 (100%)
Singapore	1977	190,600 (12.7%)	143,300 (9.5%)	331,400[11] (22.0%)	1,506,700 (100%)
	1982	389,100 (13.2%)	181,100 (6.1%)	537,200[11] (18.1%)	2,956,700 (100%)
Thailand	1977	174,000 (14.3%)	124,000 (10.2%)	197,500[3] (16.2%)	1,220,700 (100%)
	1982	228,100 (10.3%)	130,800 (5.9%)	304,300[3] (13.7%)	2,218,400 (100%)

Notes: (1) Only considers France, West Germany, Switzerland, and U.K.
        (2) Only considers U.K.
        (3) Only considers France, Italy, the Netherlands, Switzerland, and U.K.
        (4) Considers Belgium, France, Italy, Luxembourg, the Netherlands, Switzerland, and U.K.
        (5) Data unavailable since 1973.
        (6) Only considers France, West Germany, Sweden, Switzerland, and U.K.
        (7) Only considers France, West Germany, and the Netherlands.
        (8) Only considers France and West Germany.
        (9) Only considers France, Italy, the Netherlands, Sweden, Switzerland, and U.K.
       (10) Compiled from *1983 Philippine Statistical Yearbook* (Manila:NEDA) and considers Austria, Belgium, Denmark, Finland, France, West Germany, Greece, Iceland, Italy, the Netherlands, Norway, Portugal, Spain, Sweden, Switzerland, and U.K.
       (11) Considers France, West Germany, Italy, the Netherlands, U.K. and "Other European Countries" recorded in *Yearbook of Statistics Singapore 1982/1983.*

Source: United Nations' *Statistical Yearbook of Asia and the Pacific, 1983.*

TABLE IV-1a

Japanese Interests in Foreign Countries

Q: In which area or areas of the world are you most interested?

Date of Survey	5/80	5/81	6/82	6/83	6/84
Number of Respondents	2,400	2,375	2,310	2,317	2,374
Asia	37.5%	31.6%	35.4%	37.6%	34.4%
Oceania	3.5%	4.4%	5.0%	5.9%	6.0%
Middle East	30.0%	21.5%	24.2%	13.2%	24.3%
Africa	4.4%	5.1%	5.2%	5.1%	6.0%
U.S.S.R. and East Europe	14.5%	14.9%	19.6%	19.0%	24.7%
Western Europe	9.0%	12.5%	12.6%	12.7%	9.4%
North America	29.0%	40.4%	31.8%	36.9%	32.4%
Latin America	4.8%	5.0%	7.4%	5.7%	5.1%
Don't know	20.8%	20.8%	20.9%	21.6%	18.0%
Total	153.5%	156.2%	162.0%	157.8%	160.3%

Source: Compiled from *Gaiko ni Kansuru Yoron Chosa* (Survey of Public Opinion on Foreign Policy) conducted by Naikaku Sori Daijin Kambo Koho-shitsu (October 1984).

TABLE IV-1b

Japanese Perceptions, Interests and Trust of Foreign Countries

Q2 For each country, please indicate whether you are very much interested, fairly interested, not so interested, or not at all interested in its cultural aspects.

Q3 Please indicate whether you like each of the following countries very much, fairly, not so much, or not at all.

Q4 Please indicate whether each country is very trustworthy, fairly trustworthy, not so trustworthy, or not at all trustworthy.

Q5 To pursue our world interests, how important do you think it is for Japan to get along well with each of the following countries. Please indicate whether it is very important, fairly important, not so important, or not important at all.

Q6 How do you rate the following countries in terms of their future? For each country, please indicate whether it is very promising, fairly promising, not so promising, or not at all promising.

(percentage points for five image items)

	Q2 INTEREST IN CULTURE		Q3 LIKE/DISLIKE		Q4 TRUST		Q5 IMPORTANCE TO JAPAN		Q6 FUTURE PROMISE	
	POSI-TIVE	NEGA-TIVE	POSI-TIVE	NEGA-TIVE	POSI-TIVE	NEGA-TIVE	POSI-TIVE	NEGA-TIVE	POSI-TIVE	NEGA-TIVE
Korea	14.1%	80.5%	12.4%	78.2%	17.9%	69.5%	57.8%	29.6%	49.8%	34.8%
China	44.1	50.8	38.5	52.4	44.5	44.0	78.7	10.0	74.8	11.5
Philippines	6.1	88.3	10.6	79.4	13.3	73.2	37.4	49.3	24.5	59.6
Malaysia	5.7	88.5	11.6	78.2	15.3	71.1	36.7	50.1	24.9	59.3
Thailand	10.4	84.0	14.7	75.3	16.0	70.6	36.8	50.1	22.4	61.9
Indonesia	10.1	84.4	13.2	76.7	15.7	70.6	39.7	46.6	25.6	58.1
Australia	20.5	73.7	47.5	42.3	41.3	45.0	55.2	31.6	55.6	28.7
Canada	21.9	72.4	52.2	37.8	45.1	41.5	57.2	29.9	59.2	24.8
U.S.	38.7	56.1	55.5	35.6	51.8	35.9	82.1	6.9	64.3	20.8
Mexico	14.2	79.8	26.5	63.6	21.5	64.4	37.7	48.8	33.5	50.0
Brazil	12.8	81.1	27.7	62.2	29.0	57.2	48.9	38.0	41.0	43.0
U.K.	33.7	60.8	48.9	41.9	46.2	40.9	63.6	23.7	42.6	41.7
France	36.0	58.5	53.5	37.2	41.4	45.5	59.3	28.0	43.9	40.3
W. Germany	24.3	70.1	35.6	55.1	39.4	47.6	59.7	27.6	52.0	32.5
USSR	19.5	70.8	6.2	84.1	3.5	84.7	51.5	36.1	40.4	44.2

Notes: Positive: "very" + "fairly."
 Negative: "not so" + "not at all."

Source: *A Summary Report on the Syndicated Study on Japanese Perceptions of and Attitudes toward Foreign Countries* prepared by Nippon Research Center, February 1984. A survey of 1,456 respondents, November 1-5, 1983.

TABLE IV-2a

U.S. Vital Interests in Foreign Countries

Q: Tell me whether you feel the United States *does* or *does not* have a vital interest in that country.

	DOES		DOES NOT		DON'T KNOW	
	PUBLIC	LEADERS	PUBLIC	LEADERS	PUBLIC	LEADERS
Japan	82%	97%	9%	2%	9%	1%
Canada	82	95	10	4	8	1
Great Britain	80	97	11	2	9	1
Saudi Arabia	77	93	10	6	13	1
West Germany	76	98	13	1	11	1
Israel	75	92	15	8	10	*
Mexico	74	98	16	1	10	1
Egypt	66	90	19	9	15	1
People's Republic of China	64	87	19	12	17	1
France	58	84	25	15	17	1
Lebanon	55	74	27	23	18	3
Iran	51	60	36	38	13	2
Taiwan	51	44	29	54	20	2
Brazil	45	80	32	18	23	2
South Korea	43	66	36	31	21	3
Poland	43	47	38	50	19	3
Jordan	41	67	32	31	27	2
South Africa	38	54	37	43	25	3
Syria	36	46	33	52	31	2
Italy	35	79	45	20	20	1
Nigeria	32	53	35	44	33	3
India	30	57	44	40	26	3

*Less than one-half of 1%.

Source: *American Public Opinion and U.S. Foreign Policy 1983* edited by John E. Rielly (Chicago Council on Foreign Relations, 1983). A survey of 1,546 respondents, October 29-November 6, 1982.

TABLE IV-2b

U.S. Feelings Toward Foreign Countries

Q: You will notice that the boxes on this card go from the highest position of plus five (for a country you have a very favorable opinion of) all the way down to the lowest position of minus five (for a country you have a very unfavorable opinion of). How far up or down the scale would you rate the following countries?

COUNTRY	1984 (mean rating)	CHANGE FROM 1981
Canada	3.7	−0.1
Australia	3.2	+0.3
Great Britain	2.9	—(1)
Japan	1.9	+0.2
France	1.8	—(1)
West Germany	1.7	−0.3
Israel	1.3	+0.1
Brazil	1.2	−0.3
Mexico	1.1	−0.6
Egypt	1.1	−0.2
China	1.1	+0.3
Philippines	0.8	—(1)
Taiwan	0.8	−0.1
India	0.5	+0.1
South Korea	0.4	+0.2
Nigeria	0.0	+0.2
South Africa	0.0	+0.3
Saudi Arabia	−0.3	+0.1
Nicaragua	−1.4	—(1)
El Salvador	−1.4	—(1)
Cuba	−2.7	—(1)
Soviet Union	−2.8	−0.0
Iran	−3.3	—(1)

Notes: (1) Statistically insignificant.

Source: *The Gallup Report International*, Vol 11, No. 5 (October 1984). A survey of 1,518 adults 18 years and older, September 21-30, 1984.

TABLE IV-3a

Views on Future World Leaders

Q: For each of the following countries, can you tell whether, in your opinion, they will count more or less in the world, thirty years from now, than they do now?

CANADA

Ranked by Variations	+	−	O
China	68	5	+63
Canada	68	6	+62
U.S.	60	10	+50
USSR	57	10	+47
Japan	55	11	+44
West Germany	41	13	+28
Australia	35	16	+19
Israel	38	21	+17
Great Britain	35	24	+11
France	29	23	+ 6
South Africa	32	26	+ 6
Korea	27	24	+ 3
Singapore	22	25	− 3
Colombia	17	27	−10
Italy	19	29	−10
Libya	20	32	−12

UNITED STATES

	+	−	O
U.S.	82	9	+73
China	77	12	+65
Japan	69	17	+52
USSR	69	18	+51
Israel	68	20	+48
West Germany	57	24	+33
Canada	55	27	+28
South Africa	51	34	+17
Australia	46	33	+13
Great Britain	46	35	+11
Colombia	41	37	+ 4
France	40	41	− 1
Libya	40	41	− 1
Korea	36	44	− 8
Singapore	31	42	−11
Italy	30	48	−18

JAPAN

	+	−	O
China	68	2	+66
Japan	49	7	+42
U.S.	47	7	+40
USSR	38	12	+26
Australia	23	3	+20
Canada	19	5	+14
Korea	23	10	+13
West Germany	20	8	+12
South Africa	13	11	+ 2
Singapore	7	10	− 3
France	12	15	− 3
Libya	7	11	− 4
Israel	12	17	− 5
Colombia	4	9	− 5
Great Britain	13	23	−10
Italy	5	17	−12

WEST GERMANY

	+	−	O
China	79	12	+67
Japan	78	14	+64
USSR	72	21	+51
U.S.	67	23	+44
Australia	62	29	+33
Canada	61	33	+28
West Germany	60	33	+27
France	48	38	+10
South Africa	50	43	+ 7
Israel	43	50	− 7
Korea	33	54	−21
Singapore	32	58	−26
Great Britain	33	60	−27
Libya	30	59	−29
Italy	28	63	−37
Colombia	22	67	−45

FRANCE

	+	−	O
China	80	6	+74
Japan	75	10	+65
U.S.	70	13	+57
West Germany	63	13	+50
USSR	62	17	+45
Canada	53	22	+31
France	52	29	+23
Australia	45	23	+22
Israel	42	32	+10
Great Britain	42	35	+ 7
Singapore	33	27	+ 6
Korea	34	29	+ 5
South Africa	35	32	+ 3
Libya	28	36	− 8
Colombia	21	38	−17
Italy	26	50	−24

GREAT BRITAIN

	+	−	O
China	72	11	+61
USSR	70	11	+59
Japan	71	13	+58
U.S.	60	20	+40
West Germany	59	19	+40
Australia	52	26	+26
Canada	47	27	+20
Great Britain	46	37	+ 9
South Africa	40	37	+ 3
France	39	37	+ 2
Israel	38	40	− 2
Singapore	25	44	−19
Libya	25	48	−23
Italy	23	48	−25
Colombia	17	55	−38
Korea	11	51	−40

ITALY

	+	−	O
U.S.	83	13	+70
China	80	14	+66
Japan	80	14	+66
West Germany	79	15	+64
USSR	75	21	+54
Italy	70	26	+44
France	65	27	+38
Canada	62	29	+33
Australia	61	29	+32
Great Britain	59	34	+25
Israel	44	48	− 4
South Africa	41	50	− 9
Singapore	24	62	−38
Libya	26	64	−38
Colombia	20	66	−46
Korea	21	69	−48

Notes: + Percentage of persons who think that the country will count more 30 years from now.
− Percentage of persons who think that the country will count less 30 years from now.
O First percentage minus second percentage.

Source: Gallup International/International Institute of Geopolitics, *Survey Conducted in 10 Countries: The World Facing the 21st Century and the Third Industrial Revolution.* A survey conducted from February 21 to March 20, 1984 of 10,545 people including 1,046 Canadians, 1,616 Americans, 1,452 Japanese, 947 West Germans, 906 French, 1,028 Britons, and 513 Italians.

TABLE IV-3b

Europe's Trust in Other Peoples

Q: For each country, please indicate whether it is very trustworthy, fairly trustworthy, not particularly trustworthy, or not at all trustworthy.

(Average of replies from people in Community countries)

	VERY TRUST- WORTHY	FAIRLY TRUST- WORTHY	NOT PARTIC- ULARLY TRUST- WORTHY	NOT AT ALL TRUST- WORTHY	DON'T KNOW	TOTAL	TRUST INDEX[1]
Swiss	30%	41%	9%	5%	15%	100%	.68
Danes	17	41	10	4	28	100	.62
Luxembourgers	15	41	11	4	29	100	.59
Dutch	19	43	11	5	22	100	.58
Belgians	15	46	13	4	22	100	.54
Americans	24	43	16	8	9	100	.47
West Germans	18	42	17	12	11	100	.32
British	13	46	22	9	10	100	.29
Irish	10	35	19	10	26	100	.17
French	14	39	23	13	11	100	.17
Japanese	15	33	19	14	19	100	.15
Greeks	6	32	24	11	27	100	−.02
Spanish	7	34	29	13	17	100	−.07
Portuguese	5	28	25	12	30	100	−.11
Chinese	13	19	12	27	29	100	−.23
Italians	5	32	31	18	14	100	−.23
Russians	4	16	23	41	16	100	−.61

Note: (1) This index, adapted from Merritt and Puchala *(Western European Perspectives on International Affairs,* Praeger, 1968, pp. 115-117), uses the following formula: Trust = $\frac{G - B}{G + B}$, where G is the total of weighted positive replies ("very trustworthy" = 2, and "fairly trustworthy" = 1) and B is the total of weighted negative replies ("not very trustworthy" = 1, and "not trustworthy at all" = 2). Scores on the index range from −1.00 to +1.00. Differences between national scores of less than .10 should not be regarded as significant.

Source: *Euro-Barometer* 14 survey sponsored by the Commission of the European Communities (fieldwork conducted in October 1980).